'This easy-to-read book shows a brave honesty and depth of understanding that can be borne only from individual experience. It is so useful to hear Bob's point of view and the book provides helpful practical ideas for every occasion that can be easily put into practice and more importantly might spark the turning point with a difficult issue. This book shows great understanding of the fact that the size of the change is not equal to the enormity of the challenge! It reaches to the sometimes bewildering ... hear parents of children with autism spectr... y basis. The authors understand behaviour ... present the impact that the minutiae of eve... with autism and their families.'

— Chantal Blake, Clinical ... Oldham, UK

D1586467

'A jargon-free book that is easy to read. It recognises day-to-day dilemmas faced by families who have a child with autism. I was able to relate to the real-life experiences illustrated through the case studies, make sense of the practical advice and consider how it could apply to my own situation.'

— Debbie Gainsborough, parent of a child on the autism spectrum, Lancashire, UK

'Brilliant in its usefulness and accessibility to all readers, this book successfully addresses a huge issue. Life is all about change and change is one of the biggest challenges for individuals with autism spectrum disorders. It is time that an entire book deals with this important issue. Smith, Donlan and Smith accurately describe how transitions affect individuals with autism spectrum disorders. They provide real-life situations and solutions that work. Additionally, the authors provide valuable, practice-proven tools, such as scripts and signs that may be used for a variety of transition situations. *Helping Children with Autism Spectrum Conditions through Everyday Transitions* is one of those books that may be considered a "must have".'

— Dion E. Betts, Ed.D., author of Everyday Activities to Help Your Young Child with Autism Live Life to the Full *and Superintendent of Schools, Boyertown Area School District, Pennsylvania, USA*

362

Helping Children with
AUTISM
SPECTRUM
CONDITIONS
through Everyday
Transitions

by the same authors

Create a Reward Plan for Your Child with Asperger Syndrome

John Smith, Jane Donlan and Bob Smith
ISBN 978 1 84310 622 7
eISBN 978 1 84642 755 8

of related interest

Successful School Change and Transition for the Child with Asperger Syndrome
A Guide for Parents
Clare Lawrence
ISBN 978 1 84905 052 4
eISBN 978 0 85700 358 4

Making the Move
A Guide for Schools and Parents on the Transfer of Pupils with Autism Spectrum Disorders (ASDs) from Primary to Secondary School
K.I. Al-Ghani and Lynda Kenward
Illustrated by Haitham Al-Ghani
ISBN 978 1 84310 934 1
eISBN 978 1 84642 935 4

Hints and Tips for Helping Children with Autism Spectrum Disorders
Useful Strategies for Home, School, and the Community
Dion E. Betts and Nancy J. Patrick
ISBN 978 1 84310 896 2
eISBN 978 1 84642 877 7

The Complete Guide to Asperger's Syndrome
Tony Attwood
ISBN 978 1 84310 495 7 hardback
ISBN 978 1 84310 669 2 paperback
eISBN 978 1 84642 559 2

Helping Children with

AUTISM SPECTRUM CONDITIONS

through Everyday Transitions

Small Changes – Big Challenges

John Smith, Jane Donlan and Bob Smith

Jessica Kingsley *Publishers*
London and Philadelphia

Permission for quotes and case studies has been kindly granted
by family members of the children with autism.

First published in 2012
by Jessica Kingsley Publishers
116 Pentonville Road
London N1 9JB, UK
and
400 Market Street, Suite 400
Philadelphia, PA 19106, USA

www.jkp.com

Library of Congress Cataloging in Publication Data
A CIP catalog record for this book is available from the Library of Congress

British Library Cataloguing in Publication Data
A CIP catalogue record for this book is available from the British Library

ISBN 978 1 84905 275 7
eISBN 978 0 85700 572 4

Printed and bound in Great Britain

CONTENTS

INTRODUCTION

I would say that transitions could cover a whole wealth of things to do with daily living such as enabling someone to express what they want and need wherever they are…making the best use of the senses in all different kinds of environments…so many changes going on all the time…schools become a minefield of changes!

(Maureen, mother of an adult son with autism)

SMALL CHANGE = BIG CHALLENGE FOR INDIVIDUALS WITH AUTISM

The aim of this book is to bring to people's attention the challenges that regular, everyday, weekly, monthly and yearly changes bring to the lives of people with autism – the 'smaller' changes that are often overlooked because they are such a basic part of human life. They are so much a part of life that neurotypical people (that is, people who are not on the autism spectrum) probably just take them for granted and don't often give them much thought – that is, unless you live with a person who has autism and then you will see first hand just how difficult Christmas and New Year can be, for example, or how your loved one with autism struggles with the weekly change of weekend back to weekday mode and vice versa. You will probably be familiar with the confusion and distress that comes from trying to take your son or daughter away on vacation. This can be very upsetting for you because you are only trying to do something nice for your child and in doing so are causing him or her a great deal of suffering. It is always horrible to see our children suffer, but to think that we have actually caused them to feel this way is a terrible experience for us – so much so that we will probably go to great lengths to avoid causing this type of distress in the future. Hence, we avoid exposing our children to change as much as we can.

Change, no matter how positive, can be fraught with anxiety and while this is understandable, it can also be considered worth it when that change involves something as big and exciting as moving house or starting a new job. Imagine, though, feeling this level of apprehension, fear even, over something as seemingly simple as going away for the weekend or having a room decorated in your home.

For some people with autism, any change is too much change and this can have a massive impact on their lives and on the lives of the people who care about them. As we look back on how things were for us as a family before our son was able to deal with change to the degree that he is now, it is hard to believe just how completely restricted our lives were, and the effect this had on us all as individuals and as a family. That is not to say that our son doesn't struggle with change now, because he does and it is likely he always will. However, the level of anxiety that change creates in him these days is nowhere near as high as it was when he was younger and before he gained the skills he has now. In those days, we couldn't do anything spontaneously and even planned events were very anxiety-provoking for all of us. We knew that even if we were arranging to do something that our son would enjoy, there would still be a build-up of apprehension, and the fallout from this after the event often left us feeling that it just wasn't worth putting him or us through the trauma.

Often, dealing with the after-effects that change and times of transition cause for our children can be exhausting for the whole family. It can lead to conflict between the parent and the child with autism, between the child and his or her siblings, between the parents and any non-autistic siblings, and especially conflict between you as the parents or carers of the child who has an autism spectrum condition; it is not uncommon for parents of such children to separate or divorce. There is a school of thought that says that parents of children who have autism undergo a greater amount of stress and depression than parents of children who have other types of conditions, such as cerebral palsy or Down Syndrome, or even a serious or terminal illness. While things are not necessarily worse for parents of children with autism, in many cases the day-to-day stress levels are measurably higher, because these parents give everything they have to give on a practical, physical and emotional level, but receive very little back in return. Children with autism are often unable to express their feelings to their parents and so may come across as unemotional, uncaring and unappreciative of the effort that their parents are putting into the relationship. However, just because our children may find it hard to let us know they care about us doesn't mean they don't love us; they deserve every bit of support that we can give them to help them express their emotions to the best of their ability, and to establish and maintain relationships. One way we can enable them to cope with their lives and relationships is to help them deal with change, from the bigger, more life-changing events such as leaving school, to the smaller changes and periods of transition that we discuss in this book. Helping your child to deal with these changes should have a positive impact on both the child and the rest of the family.

We wrote this book because we were unable to find any information about dealing with the smaller, more regular changes of life. Lots of information exists about dealing with the bigger changes, such as moving from primary to senior school, and this is very helpful. However, we noticed that our son was struggling every weekend and especially every Monday morning with the change of routine. He loves vacations, but the anxiety before and after a vacation was causing immense problems for the family. He just couldn't cope with all the change and this was played out in his behaviour. It became obvious to us that we needed to be proactive when it came to helping our son face these regular changes that were creating a state of almost constant anxiety in him. We went through some very difficult times and had some horrible experiences when our son was faced with even very small changes. We used the reward plan that is described in our first book, *Create a Reward Plan for Your Child with Asperger Syndrome*, and this did help, but using in addition the transition techniques described in this book helped us to give our son a real insight into change, how it works and how it can be managed for 'damage limitation'. In fact, our son doesn't just cope with change nowadays, he even enjoys some changes! He does still struggle at times, and some of the changes he finds hard are even 'smaller' than the ones this book was written for, but on the whole his attitude towards, and relationship with change is much more positive than it was before we began using the transition techniques with him.

We worked together as a family to develop these techniques and strategies to help our son, and this in turn helped us all. Because of this success, we decided to write this book in the hope that we could help other families get through times of change as smoothly and calmly as possible. When you work together as a family, you can overcome some of the difficulties and challenges of Asperger Syndrome, relax more and even enjoy many of its positive features. The techniques as described are applicable to a child with Asperger Syndrome, such as our son.

However, with some adjustment they are just as appropriate for a child with more classic autism.

Our aim in writing this book is to explore some of the challenges and difficulties faced by people with autism living in a predominantly neurotypical world. As neurotypical people are not going to change their ways to make life easier for people with autism, then those with autism, who are in the minority, have to try to adapt their behaviour to fit in, thus avoiding the alternative: fear, anxiety and confusion. We are not trying to change people with autism, rather, aiming to help them cope better in the neurotypical world, thus making their lives easier and less stressful.

We hope that you enjoy reading this book, and find it useful. Take time to familiarize yourself with the transition techniques, and practise them with your son or daughter. They may take some time to get used to, and to start working, but don't give up at the first hurdle, as you will eventually gain some very positive results by putting in the effort and working consistently with your child. We wish you lots of success.

On a final note: as this book was written over a period of time, our son was at first being home educated and then started college, so both of these are mentioned throughout the book, depending which issue we are trying to highlight. Also, we use the terms 'parents', 'your child' and 'your son or daughter' for ease of writing, but of course we are also aiming this book at carers, guardians, professionals, educators and anyone else who is involved in the child's life.

PART ONE

---- · · · ·

ISSUES RELATED TO CHANGE

1
AUTISM AND ASPERGER SYNDROME

Brief Overview

I don't even care about the academic stuff...I just want her to make friends, to be able to ask for something in a shop, get on a bus, even get a job when she grows up...the things that most of us do automatically...

(Father of a ten-year-old daughter with autism)

Autism is a very complicated condition. It ranges from Kanner's, or classic, autism, to Asperger Syndrome or High Functioning Autism. People who have classic autism may have extreme symptoms, such as not being able to make eye contact at all and not being able to speak or to communicate their needs in other ways, and may need an enormous amount of support in their day-to-day activities. They may need help with their personal care as well as with their social and communication needs. This can also be true of people who have higher functioning autism. They may have average or above average IQs, but can still struggle significantly with caring for themselves and with their interactions with others. Asperger Syndrome is often described as 'mild autism', and maybe to the parents of children with classic autism this seems to be the case, but as parents of a child with Asperger Syndrome we can say that there is nothing 'mild' about its symptoms. Individuals on the autism spectrum are exactly that – individuals – and the degree to which autism affects them, and the form that this takes, will vary from person to person.

THE TRIAD OF IMPAIRMENTS

It is generally agreed that the defining aspects of autism are the difficulties that individuals have, to varying degrees, in three specific areas: social interaction and social understanding; communication skills (verbal and non-verbal); and flexibility of thought and behaviour. Let's look at each of these in a little more detail.

Difficulties in social interaction and social understanding

People with autism may find it difficult to interact with others, and may not understand social situations or what is expected of them; a simple example of this is letting a door go as you walk through it, instead of holding it open for the person behind you. This is a basic social skill that neurotypical people will learn probably without even being taught. People with autism, therefore, may come across as rude and ignorant, when the truth is they just haven't picked up on the social etiquette of holding the door open for someone coming behind them. People with autism are often unaware of the social aspects of the society we live in; they can be completely oblivious to the social culture going on around them and only focus on their own immediate needs and wants. It may be that they have some awareness of social etiquette and expectations, but they may think these silly and unnecessary; they may put more value on the truth than on sparing someone's feelings, for example. It is possible to teach correct social interaction, such as saying hello or shaking hands when meeting someone in a more formal setting, but teaching social understanding is more difficult. Despite their often high IQs, people with autism spectrum condition aren't always able to take something they have learned in one situation and transfer it to another, and so gaining skills in social interaction and social understanding is often a life-long, ongoing work in progress for them. It is often the case that we teach our children how to act and comply with the correct social behaviour in one setting, and expect them to know that this is how they should behave in similar social settings, only then to see them struggle completely when that situation changes even slightly: for example, sitting quietly in the cinema to watch a film, and then having to go through the whole thing again next time you take them to the cinema because it's a different film, or a different cinema, or you are sitting in different seats. Or you may have taught them to say 'please' and 'thank you', or wait their turn in a queue in a shop, but they may not understand *why* they are doing or saying these things, other than Mum or Dad has promised them chocolate if they do! This may be one reason why it is so hard for someone who has autism to comply with social etiquette; if you don't understand why you are doing something you are less likely to recognize situations where you need to do this again, and to do so of your own volition.

Difficulties in communication skills (verbal and non-verbal)

The communication difficulties experienced by people who have autism are very wide and varied, but the fact is that with autism spectrum condition there will be some level of difficulty when it comes to communicating with others. It may be difficult for someone with autism to initiate a conversation, to join in an ongoing conversation, or even to respond appropriately to a conversation initiated by someone else. Non-verbal communication accounts for a massive amount of our understanding of other people and of their intentions towards us. People who have an autism spectrum condition, whether this be classic or High Functioning Autism, will have difficulty in reading other people's body language and their facial expressions, and this will obviously lead to confusion on their part and a tendency to 'get it wrong'. It is well documented that some people with autism have a 'special interest', a subject that they are totally fascinated by and absorbed in, and sometimes they will talk for long periods of time on this topic. The problem is that other people may not always want to listen, and the person with autism is probably not skilled in picking up the non-verbal cues that the 'listener' is no longer listening, and wants the talker to be quiet.

Of course, some individuals with autism may have no (or very little) speech and be completely unable to make their needs known. If in addition they cannot understand what people mean when they speak to them, they can become stressed, and indeed feel very vulnerable. An example of this vulnerability is the bullying that so many people with autism spectrum condition experience. They may be befriended by someone who is in fact having a laugh at their expense, or even harming them in some obvious way, yet not realize what the nature of the relationship actually is and really believe this person is a friend. Parents often report that their young person with autism has been in trouble at school or with the police because others have exploited his or her vulnerability and led the young person into doing something wrong or even illegal.

This lack of understanding regarding social and communication skills is not necessarily indicative of lower intelligence – far from it – but it is clear that we need to help our young people recognize body language and other non-verbal cues in order to teach them about friendships and other relationships, and to help them get the best out of their experiences of communication.

Difficulty with flexibility of thought and behaviour

People with autism spectrum condition can be 'rigid' in their thinking, often finding it hard to see someone else's point of view. They can also be very resistant to any type of change, no matter how seemingly insignificant, becoming distressed when their expectations or routine are upset or altered in some way. Even the most flexible of people with autism may find some changes just too much to cope with. They might, for example, tolerate a big change, such as going through the transition from school to college, yet become distressed if their regular breakfast cereal is not available, or the programme they always watch at 7 pm on a Wednesday evening has been cancelled for some reason.

Coping with such changes, and learning to appreciate another's point of view, require flexibility of thinking – a skill that can be learned, but only with time, patience and consistency. And, as with the learning of social behaviour, the flexibility learned in one specific situation won't necessarily be transferable to a similar situation. Learning to be less rigid and more flexible tends to be another on-going project for people with autism.

DIFFERENCE OR DISABILITY?

Autism is often seen as a social and communication disorder or disability. While some people are comfortable with the idea of autism as a disability, others – often those with Asperger Syndrome – do not see themselves as having a disability, and may consider some aspects of their diagnosis as a distinct advantage in lots of areas of their lives. For example, they may appreciate their intelligence, their skills and knowledge in particular areas, their honesty and straightforwardness, their attention to detail, their unique sense of humour, and so on. Who is to say where difference ends and disability begins?

2
CHANGE

With autism comes a whole heap of issues…transition, routine, repetition, and everyday living can be so awkward…

(Mother of Oliver, aged five)

THE CHALLENGE OF CHANGE

Change for most of us can be exciting, sometimes frustrating, and at worst, a bit of a challenge, particularly when it involves major upheaval, such as moving house or starting a new job. For people with autism spectrum condition, however, any change, big or small, can be daunting. It can cause great confusion, fear and distress, which in turn can have an impact on their behaviour. They may find each day a struggle as they try to deal with the changes that are a regular feature of everyday life. To minimize their constant anxiety, people with autism strongly resist all this change and strive for 'sameness' in their lives. This need for sameness could be because the world can be such a scary place when you have autism. If you struggle to understand society and how it works, how people interact with each other and why, and the social rules and etiquette; if you struggle to understand your own emotions and those of other people; and if you often feel as though you have landed on an alien planet where very little makes sense to you and you feel that you just don't fit in, then it is not surprising that you might insist that those things you are used to and feel okay with should stay the same. Knowing exactly what to expect can help a person feel safe and secure.

Many of the changes that challenge a person with autism are the sort of day-to-day occurrences that a neurotypical person would barely notice: the transition from weekday to weekend mode and back again; the clocks going forward or back one hour at the beginning and end of summer; a different jam at breakfast time; a picture being moved, or a new lamp added in a room. The possibilities are endless. Here is a list of some of the smaller, regularly occurring changes that can cause so much distress to a person with autism:

- public holidays or festivals, such as Christmas, Eid or Diwali

- vacations or weekends away

- the change of seasons

- the person's birthday

- changes of bedtime

- tradespeople coming to the house

- decorating the house

- a family member going away, into hospital, etc.

- new clothes or shoes

- taking a different route to school.

Changes such as these, and many others, have caused Bob to struggle on a regular basis as the year progresses from New Year through to Christmas. Like many families affected by autism, we did our best to help our child cope with what were to us small, quite insignificant changes. To Bob, they were clearly insurmountable and to be avoided at all costs. When he was faced with a change, we were faced with his distress, confusion and aggression, and our own inability to deal with these. We often felt powerless, useless and inadequate as parents. It was hard for us to understand why nothing in his room could ever be touched or moved, even to clean underneath! It was bewildering when Mum or Dad attempted to dust the fireplace, only to have Bob fly into a rage because we had fractionally moved one of the dragons in his collection. He was unable to cope with this tiniest of changes – a change that would have gone unnoticed by anyone else.

. . . .

Case study – Ryan
Ryan finds small transitions as well as major ones extremely difficult to cope with and these changes have become much more stressful for him as he gets older. Some of the smaller changes that Ryan finds difficult include coming home from school or returning from an outing, lining up at break-times to return to his class and

generally going from one place to another, even when he is in familiar surroundings and with people he knows well. Holidays, vacations and weekends are also difficult for him to cope with. It is often a real struggle to know how best to help Ryan during these stressful times...

Case study – Robert

When Robert was young, even the tiniest change in his routine or environment was enough to send him into a state of panic, which would often lead to a big emotional outburst. This could be something as simple as moving one of his toys from the place where he liked to keep it, or rearranging ornaments or furniture in the house. In fact, recently he became very distressed when his mum suggested moving some plant pots from the patio to a position in front of the shed. He grew angry quickly and said, 'But that's not how we have the shed; it doesn't have plants in front of it.' Most 13-year-old boys wouldn't have given the shed or the plant pots a second thought!

But to Robert it was just too much change.

Case study – Bob

When Bob's family moved house, it was a massive change for all of them. For years he would grow angry at the very mention of the idea of moving house. His parents spent a lot of time talking to him about the differences and similarities between their current house and the new house, such as, 'The new house will have more rooms.' Eventually, he was able to express his anxieties about the move: he was upset about not being able to take the insects from the house and garden that he'd become very fond of! This was overcome by taking photos and filming them. Bob, like most people with autism, had found it very hard to recognize and to express his feelings, and change does evoke a lot of mixed feelings and emotions.

These case studies illustrate how significant any change, big or small, can be for people who have autism. The level of anxiety they endure when faced with even the smallest change can be the same as (or worse than) that experienced by a neurotypical person dealing with major, life-changing situations, such as getting married or starting a new job. But neurotypical people, at the same time as feeling nervous or fearful, also experience a level of excitement or anticipation. They will also have strategies to cope with their strong feelings. People with autism, on the other hand, often don't recognize what they are actually feeling, and therefore don't have any coping strategies. This is why techniques that can help them through periods of transition are so important.

THE BENEFITS OF CHANGE

After all, change isn't all bad. Without it, we are stuck in a dull cycle of routine and sameness, and unable to make progress in our lives. Here are just some of the benefits that change and new situations can bring to our lives:

- the opportunity for new and different experiences

- stimulation, and educational opportunities

- increased self-confidence and self-esteem

- the confidence to try new things, once we have successfully negotiated one change

- the possibility of meeting people and making new friends

- a more varied, interesting and fun life!

It seems unfair that individuals with autism spectrum condition should be denied these advantages because of their overwhelming desire for sameness. This is how we felt when we developed the transition techniques that have worked so well for our son and for us as a family. We have used these techniques to deal with the bigger changes in our son's life, but in fact we created them to deal with the constant, smaller changes that we face every day. While we have mentioned many of these already, you will probably think of many more.

When you think what is required of children just to get through every single day, with the numerous changes and transitions that occur all the time, it is not surprising that their continual state of anxiety about these changes leads to 'meltdowns' and emotional outbursts. We want to help you and your child become more confident, and less anxious and stressed with all these everyday changes. We hope that, as a consequence, your child displays less challenging behaviours, and will be equipped to handle change throughout his or her life, even without you there for guidance.

Using the transition techniques, simple though they are, we have got closer than we ever thought possible to our goal of helping Bob accept change as an inevitable part of life. In the past 12 months, our son has gone from being home educated and never venturing out on his own, to going to mainstream college. He catches a bus there and back on his own, and has made new friends without Mum or Dad's support or influence. He is a year younger than most of the other students in his year, but has still managed to achieve distinctions in the six units he has been studying – despite his dyslexia and dyspraxia. And he has done all this on his own, without the aid of a support worker. There's no doubt he does still struggle with change – perhaps he always will to some extent – but now he has greater awareness of his problems, and has gained the confidence and skills to allow change into his life. He recognizes that change, though sometimes scary and unwelcome, can be a good thing; he also understands that he can still benefit from an increase in confidence and a sense of achievement even when things don't go according to plan.

INTRODUCING CHANGE SLOWLY

Wherever possible, it is important to introduce change slowly and carefully, in order to minimize any negative reactions in your child. Two of our major successes by doing this have been to get Bob used to Mum going out without him, for example, to the gym, or for a drink with friends; and his 'bedtime plan' (details of which can be found in our first book, *Create a Reward Plan for Your Child with Asperger Syndrome*). The bedtime plan took many months to be successfully navigated, but it is one of the best things we ever did. In fact, it quite literally changed our lives. Previously, Bob had gone to bed in Mum's bed, and she had to stay with him until he fell asleep – sometimes not until 3 am. By implementing the bedtime plan gradually and consistently, Mum was eventually able to sit downstairs in the evening – sometimes even go out! – and have her bed to herself (the first time in ten years); and of course, get some much-needed sleep. It is sad, looking back, to think about those long, difficult times, and hard to believe that there was ever a time that we couldn't get our son to sleep – especially as these days we can't get him to wake up! Mum says to him, 'You could sleep through an earthquake', and on one occasion he really did!

We hope that this little story from our lives might give any of you who are struggling with your child's sleep patterns some hope. There *is* light at the end of this very long tunnel.

Of course, while it can be much less stressful all round to introduce changes slowly and consistently, there are times that this isn't possible. Sometimes change happens suddenly, without warning – for example, a parent is called away, and the child has to be looked after by someone else. This is where practice is so important. The more practice you have in using the transition techniques for changes you can anticipate, the easier it will be to implement them on occasions where you have little notice.

Bob's comments

I'm not a psychologist. I don't know why change is hard. Stuff is just the way it is. Change feels hard. That's all it feels like.

Mum moved the bench that I sit on at the dining table to the other side of the table to give more room. She wanted to use this as an example of how I struggle with small change, because I like to sit on the bench but can't now it's no longer on my side. I don't want to change the side where I sit so now I have to sit on the chair. However, Mum always complains that the bench is uncomfortable but she sits on it now because she doesn't want to change sides, so I guess it's not only people with autism who find small changes difficult!

Change at short notice is the worst kind. Most people find this slightly difficult, but if you have autism it is even more difficult. Even if you know there is a perfectly good reason for this change, it doesn't make it any easier to deal with it. Sometimes, something as simple as having to go out when you hadn't thought you'd have to can be a very difficult thing. What makes it even harder is that most people, even if they are slightly put out by the short notice of the change, are much better able to deal with it and therefore do not realize how hard it is for the person with autism. Quite often the person with autism won't even realize how hard it is for themselves. It might sound patronizing and even condescending to say, but it is a fact that people with autism find it hard to recognize their own emotions and this can make a situation even more confusing and irritating for them. There is no way to avoid these kinds of changes altogether, but if possible it is much better to stick to the plans you have already made – you just need to think them through more before you finalize them – but as I say, this is not always possible and some plans will have to be changed at short notice. If this is the case, then the person with autism needs to remember that in reality it's not that big a deal and there is probably a good reason for the change. This is not always easy to do, but it gets easier with time. The people involved who do not have autism will need to remember and try to understand how difficult it actually is for the person wih autism. If they do not try to do this then the situation is sure to end badly for all involved. Equally, the person with autism will eventually have to face up to the fact that they are overreacting to what is a minor event, even though it may be major in their mind.

Some changes are a lot bigger, such as changes of routine. Even if you are able to see them coming a long way off, they may still have a profound effect upon your life if you don't handle them properly. This might include, for example, a serious change of routine such as going to a new school or college, or being on vacation from school, work or college. Obviously, being on vacation is a good thing, but everything changes: the time you get up, what you do after you get up, how you spend your day and what time you go to bed. You may also not be seeing people who you were used to seeing every day of the school or college year. All of these things can be very difficult and are not easy to overcome by any means. What makes them even more difficult is the fact that after six weeks or so you have to change back. One way of dealing with this is to do what I did; I have a very big interest and passion in film, so for a few weeks before I broke up from college I bought several DVDs that I had been wanting to watch for a long time but decided not to watch them until I had finished college. So I already had my first week of the holidays planned almost a month in advance! This meant that when the time came it didn't feel like a change in routine, as I had planned out exactly what I was going to do for the first couple of days. Now I am just glad of the break and the chance to watch all of the films!

3

EMOTIONS

Sometimes his expression of his own feelings is inappropriate, such as laughing at things that other people would be shocked by. However, when given an opportunity to comment on the situation, he seems to understand it on an intellectual level but not know how to respond on an emotional level; an example of this is if someone hurts themselves…

(Father of Bob, aged 16)

Times of change and transition can evoke a lot of mixed feelings in all of us. Emotions can run high. These can be positive or negative emotions, but if you are a person with autism it won't necessarily matter which, as the outcome can be the same – anxiety, worry and even fear can result from an inability to recognize and deal with the emotions that change brings. This in turn can lead to behaviours that are not always deemed appropriate or acceptable. This chapter looks at how change can impact on the emotions, and therefore the behaviour, of people with autism.

In *The Complete Guide To Asperger Syndrome*, Tony Attwood says that Theory of Mind is 'being able to recognize and understand the thoughts, beliefs, desires and intentions of other people in order to make sense of their behaviour and predict what they are going to do next' (p.112). He says that the person with Asperger Syndrome does not 'recognize or understand the cues that indicate the thoughts or feelings of the other person at a level expected for someone of that age' (p.112).

Often, people with autism, including Asperger Syndrome, do not recognize or understand their own feelings, either. It would seem that there is a delay in developing these skills and maybe they never will develop as fully as they would in a neurotypical person. However, it is not that people with autism or Asperger Syndrome can't feel, sympathize or empathize, it is just much, much harder for them to do so, or to express these feelings. It can be that the will is there, but often the skill isn't.

Tony Attwood also points out that there is an increased risk of mood disorders, such as depression, in teenagers with Asperger Syndrome. This may be hard to detect if they are struggling to show their emotions, and their facial expressions are difficult to read. Their underlying depression may come out as anger, or they may become even more quiet and withdrawn than usual. If you have a teenager who has an autism spectrum condition such as Asperger Syndrome, then it may be worthwhile your reading up on mood disorders so that you are armed with the knowledge you may need if depression does become an issue for your child.

RECOGNIZING AND CONSIDERING ANOTHER PERSON'S EMOTIONS

As well as struggling to understand and express their own feelings, most people with autism spectrum condition have problems when it comes to understanding the facial expressions, body language and vocal intonations of others. Non-verbal communication plays a major part in our interactions with, and social understanding of, other people. Having an impairment in the recognition of non-verbal communication, therefore, could be likened to being in a foreign country where you don't understand the language, the culture or people's gestures. This would be frustrating and distressing as you start to feel more and more out of your depth. It is possible that people who have an autism spectrum condition experience these feelings of frustration and vulnerability when they are trying to process and decipher other people's facial expressions and body language. Add to this a difficulty in expressing emotions appropriately, or making the right facial expression, and some serious misunderstandings will inevitably result.

The following case study illustrates how difficult it can be for someone with autism to recognize and consider another person's emotions, especially when his or her own are heightened.

Case study – Bob
RECOGNIZING AND DEALING WITH HIS OWN EMOTIONS

Bob can be calm one minute and incredibly angry the next. There seems to be no build-up to his anger, though there clearly is – he just isn't able to express the developing emotions, and as his face is often blank, his parents are not able to detect them. Sometimes it's as though there are no 'in-between' feelings, just calm, then angry. His level of anger is usually way out of proportion to the situation. An example of this is when Bob and his mum are walking along the road and Mum can't hear what Bob has said because of the traffic noise. Bob gets very angry straight away and shouts, 'Learn to listen!' extremely loudly. His anger is way too severe for such a simple and everyday occurrence. Of course, there are other reasons for this extreme response, not just the fact that he hasn't been heard. Sensory overload probably plays a part here, too. But this example does highlight how Bob is unable to deal successfully with his developing emotions, and so resorts to the same one each time he is stressed, confused, overwhelmed, frustrated, irritated or even sad – every negative emotion he feels is expressed as anger.

He went to school until he was seven. At school, he was frequently praised for being quiet and compliant. Apart from a couple of minor incidents, his behaviour was always exemplary. However, as soon as he came out of school and saw his mum, things would change. Immediately, he would push or pull her in a very controlling way. He would be snappy and often outright aggressive. His feelings, which he suppressed all day at school, manifested only as tics in the playground. But as soon as he saw his mum, all of his emotion was released, and since he had no way of saying exactly how he was feeling, it came out as anger.

RECOGNIZING AND DEALING WITH OTHER PEOPLE'S EMOTIONS

If Bob and his mum have a disagreement he can never just let the argument go. It has to be resolved there and then, in that moment. He can't even bear for her to have a few minutes alone to calm down. He becomes very distressed and won't stop arguing until she says that she feels fine now and that all negative feelings are gone. Of course, this is impossible for her to do, and so often ends up in him crying, shouting and throwing things. When any type of conflict or disagreement takes place between Bob and his mum, it seems he can't listen and talk things through at that time. He has to be right all of the time, and is completely unable to see Mum's point of view when he is angry and upset. Even if his mum is crying or saying, 'This needs to stop now. I am getting very upset and so are you', Bob is unable to acknowledge Mum's feelings. It's as though he can't even see that Mum is upset; or worse, that he can see it but just doesn't care. This isn't the case, though. He does care, but he struggles so much to express this.

One mother wrote in a magazine article that her son showed absolutely no response when she was upset. She said, 'That's the thing about autism; I can sit on the sofa next to him, bawling my eyes out, and he will just carry on watching *Blue Peter* as though I'm not even there.' Bob's mum knows exactly what she means!

Recently, however, Bob has started to come to Mum after a falling-out and try to sort out the issue. Unfortunately, his way of doing this is to go over the argument and say why he was right and she was wrong. If Mum is still crying, he will say something like, 'You can stop crying now. I've apologized, haven't I?' If Mum is unable to stop crying he will start to get angry again and shout at her to stop, because 'the argument's over now'. This happened recently; Bob came into the lounge to apologize, but Mum was so distressed by the falling-out they'd had that she couldn't stop sobbing. She was gulping in air and finding it hard to breathe. Bob had absolutely no idea how to comfort Mum, and shouted at her because, as far as he was concerned, he had said sorry. Now she needed to say sorry, and then all feelings of upset or distress would just disappear, because the argument was over. He had no concept at all of how bad his mum must have been feeling in order for her to get to the point of uncontrollable sobbing.

HOW DOES THIS DIFFICULTY IN RECOGNIZING AND EXPRESSING EMOTIONS IMPACT ON OUR CHILDREN AT TIMES OF CHANGE?

Change can bring out strong and often mixed feelings in everyone, especially at times of major change and transition, such as changing schools or jobs, or moving house. These changes can understandably create feelings of fear, anxiety, excitement, apprehension and a whole range of other emotions. Most people would be able to understand what they are feeling, and be able to articulate some, if not all, of these feelings to others. For someone with autism, this would be a very difficult thing to do. It's hard enough for them to recognize when they are feeling just one emotion; mixed emotions often just don't make any sense at all!

When people are experiencing strong emotions and they are not able to recognize the feelings, or make those feelings known to others, there is an impact on their behaviour. There is always a reason behind any negative behaviour displayed by our children. They may not be able to tell us what they are feeling or why they are behaving the way they are – often it is guess work on our part. If children are experiencing a period of transition, even something as minor as weekday to weekend mode or vice versa, it is possible that this will have a confusing effect on their emotions, and ultimately, their behaviour.

Bob's comments

Sometimes it can be hard for anyone to understand how they are feeling, but this is even more so for someone with Asperger Syndrome or autism. This can quite often lead to conflict with people around you and can also leave you even more confused about what exactly it is you are feeling. It can also be difficult to recognize other people's feelings and emotions. Most of the time, other people will not understand this, so you might come across as emotionless or uncaring even if this is not the case. Not being able to recognize your emotions can cause a lot of trouble as you may express what you are feeling in different ways, and if people do not know that you are upset or angry they may not understand why you are acting the way you are. Sometimes it is actually the other way round, and people with autism have heightened emotions. For example, they might be very quick to anger, and get angry over what somebody else perceives as a very small and meaningless thing. However, just because you are having heightened emotions doesn't mean that you are able to recognize and understand what you are feeling – the opposite is probably the case!

If you are getting angry, you need to have certain strategies in place to help you to deal with your anger before it gets out of hand. It is never easy for anyone to deal with their anger, and that is why you must find ways to prevent yourself from getting angry, first and foremost. Once you are angry, you won't be thinking clearly. The scripts, signs and sketches that come later on in the book will be a very good way of helping you deal with your anger.

Obviously, you can't go through your life not getting angry, so one of the most important things is to make sure you don't overreact when you are angry, such as ensuring you don't lash out or break things. If you do this, you will feel better after the argument than you would if you had broken something or lashed out at someone. Obviously, there will be arguments that occur when you need to lash out at someone, but these won't be with family or close friends. It may be that someone picks a fight with you and you are trying to defend yourself; then you might have to hit someone. Even in those situations it will be important for you to keep control of your anger so that you do not end up behaving like Tommy DeVito in *Goodfellas*. For those of you who have not seen the film, the character of Tommy overreacts and takes offence over the smallest of things that other people don't even notice. His reactions are often violent and cause trouble for him, his friends and everyone involved. His anger and inability to control his own temper often end in people being badly hurt or even killed. Although this is an extreme example, it is still worth remembering that people with autism can actually act like this. It is usually on a much smaller and less violent scale, but they flare up seemingly out of the blue, believing that somebody has said or done something to deliberately annoy them, when in fact the person has no idea they have done anything wrong. An example from my life would be when Mum asked me to come and help her minimize a window on her lap top. This is probably the most simple thing you can do on a computer, even easier than copying and pasting or checking your emails. That is why it infuriated me that she had been using computers for over ten years and had no idea how to do this! I thought she would have at least wandered on to it accidently during that time, but apparently not! But as far as she was concerned she needed help in being taught how to do it. I had to show her three times, and this just made me more and more angry. I snapped at her and called her an idiot and said she was stupid for not being able to do it, and likened it to living in a house for ten years and not knowing how to open a door. As I was doing this, she was trying to defend herself, saying it was complicated and she needed help. The more she said this, the angrier I got at her refusal to accept that it was actually a very simple task to perform. I banged my fist on the table and shouted at her and she refused to help me to work on my book after that. So this is an example of something Mum did that she didn't even know would annoy me, and me getting very angry about it – the anger was probably way out of proportion to the situation! This had negative consequences for me and Mum, and meant that we could not continue with what we were doing. This is what is known in our house as the Tommy DeVito effect! Although these examples are all about emotions, for people with autism, some of the things that can stir up emotions are changes, on a big or small scale. If then you are not able to handle these emotions, they can come across as anger, or be misinterpreted by other people. Being able to handle change is a good first step to being able to control and understand your emotions.

Even people who don't have autism can struggle to understand their emotions. Autism really is just a collection of extreme forms of the sorts of behaviours that most people exhibit and go through anyway. It's very important to remember how much effort it takes to stay constantly in touch with your own emotions, and how difficult it may be in certain situations to face up to what you are really feeling. Some people may be embarrassed about being upset and not wish to show it to other people. (This, by the way, is definitely not something that is confined to people with autism.) At Christmas or on my birthday, when I unwrap my presents, however happy I am with them I never really show much emotion. I am not sure why this is, but it doesn't really matter which present I am unwrapping, I always react the same (I refer to this again in Chapter 7, 'Public Holidays and Festivals').

Anyway, sometimes it can be good not to be *too* emotional, as people who are excessive with their emotions can be annoying – jumping up and down and squealing when they are happy, or sitting round crying when they are miserable – so it is important to find the right balance between recognizing and expressing your emotions, and not forcing your emotions on other people when they don't really care.

4
SENSORY OVERLOAD

Because non-autistic people have innate social antennae, we are unaware of the numerous and subtle changes and transitions that are going on around us. But autistic people are experiencing these all the time…some or many of these changes may seem quite terrifying!

(Maureen, mother of an adult son with autism)

My son is 23 and has severe autism, severe learning difficulties and challenging behaviour. He wasn't born with challenging behaviour, but he has gone through so many changes and transitions in his life where there has been an inadequate knowledge of his autism, that he must have experienced immense frustrations, fear and confusion…

(Mother of an adult son with autism)

SENSORY SENSITIVITY

The effect on the senses is a very important part of autism, but one that is often overlooked. Not enough is known about how or why the senses are so acutely affected by autism, but there is no doubt that they are.

Often, times of change or transition can expose children to increased sensory stimulation; for example, when going on holiday they may have to go to a train station. Here, there will be lots of noise: trains, announcements and people bustling about. There may also be lots of new or different sights or smells for them to contend with. At festival times, they may be exposed to additional noise, different foods and increased social visits. The house may look different if it's been decorated; parents may be off work. This is a lot of change for children with autism to cope with. Therefore, we have decided to include a chapter on senses and how a sensory overload can affect your child's behaviour.

Children with autism can have increased or decreased sensory sensitivity. They can be:

- hypersensitive: feeling something more than a neurotypical person would

- hyposensitive: feeling something less than a neurotypical person would.

It is possible for someone with autism to be both hyper- and hyposensitive at the same time. For example, they could be hypersensitive to the feel of material on skin, but barely feel the hot or cold weather. They can be incredibly sensitive to sound, touch, smell and often sight, for example, noticing tiny details that other people never would, and yet spend so long focusing on the trivia that they miss the bigger picture.

SELF-STIMULATION

Often, people with autism may try to stimulate their own senses using techniques such as flapping their hands or spinning things. One child went through a period of pressing sharp things into the skin on the back of his hands. This wasn't self-harming, but done from a desire to feel some sort of deep pressure. This need for deep pressure stimulation often comes along with dyspraxia; sensory deprivation is a part of dyspraxia, and often children with autism have co-existing conditions such as dyspraxia or dyslexia. Children with dyspraxia often need firmness or pressure and may wrap themselves up tightly in blankets, for example, sleeping inside a quilt cover like a sleeping bag. Dyspraxia affects fine and gross motor skills, and the sense of where the body is in relation to other things, so affecting balance (vestibular) and proximity (proprioceptive). Children may, therefore, fall over a lot, bump into things or get too close to other people without realizing. It can also affect children's awareness of their own strength. Physiotherapy can help with all of this (see the Resource section for how to find out more about dyslexia and dyspraxia).

Children with autism often have tics, such as clenching and unclenching muscles. This can sometimes be associated with Tourette's Syndrome. The stereotypical idea of Tourette's Syndrome is of a person shouting out obscenities, swearing and spitting. Of course, this can happen to a percentage of people with the condition, but there is a lot more to Tourette's Syndrome than this. If your child has tics it may be worth looking into Tourette's as a possible cause for these. Professionals were never able to say in our son's case whether the tics were Tourette's related or autism related or both (he has a diagnosis of both conditions). They were a big part of his life when he was younger, but the tics have certainly lessened over the years (see the Resource section for how to find out more about Tourette's Syndrome).

It is important to remember that all self-stimulatory behaviour will serve a purpose, and though that purpose may not be immediately evident, it is a good idea to observe your child to try to discover what he or she may be getting from the experience. If the behaviour displayed would be considered 'naughty' in a neurotypical child, such as throwing or always putting things into water, it is worth trying to find a similar, more appropriate activity for your child if you can.

SENSORY OVERLOAD

Sensory overload is when the child's senses are heightened to a point where he or she becomes anxious, uncomfortable, scared or overwhelmed.

Case study – Bob

When Bob was a new baby, his grandad used to get cross at the idea of having to be quiet when the baby was asleep. He always said, 'We had four babies and we were never quiet for you! We could vacuum around you and you wouldn't wake up.'

He had to see for himself just how sensitive his new grandson actually was to noise. He would wake up as soon as his mum moved: she just needed to walk across the room or open the door! He rarely slept, except on her knee, which meant she never got a break when he was asleep. It was exhausting for her. She could barely even breathe without waking him up, let alone get the vacuum cleaner out!

Case study – Robert

Robert cannot bear new clothes, and his parents often waste money on things that never get worn! He just can't stand the feel of new things. It takes ages for him to get used to a new item and sometimes, most times in fact, he won't even try. At the moment, he has two nice new jackets hanging in his wardrobe, and he is wearing a scruffy old one that he won't part with. The new ones have never been worn.

He is also sensitive to physical contact and will only hug with his mum. Because of his need for deep pressure (Robert also has dyspraxia), he often hugs too hard and can hurt by accident. He is always trying to playfight and wrestle with his mum, but he is just too big and strong now! He spends a lot of time doing this with his dad and he loves this type of physical contact.

Case study – Bob

Bob can't stand sun cream to be applied. He usually cooperates when on holiday abroad, probably because the pay off (sea, waves, sand, ice-cream) is so big! At home, it is a challenge even to get him into the garden in summer. He wears long-sleeved clothes and will only put sun cream on his face, neck and ears and the backs of his hands. This is always done under protest and after creating a lot of stress for his parents. He moans about wearing a sun hat and glasses at home, but on holiday he just gets on with it. In winter, he wears a thin coat and no hat, scarf or gloves. People have often commented, especially when he was younger, implying that his mum is a 'bad mum', but she is past caring now about what other people think, and says, 'Having a child with autism quickly gets you to that point!'

It is important to remember that any sensory sensitivity that makes your child physically uncomfortable (such as clothes that are irritating) could have a negative effect on his or her behaviour. Food can also be a big issue for some children with autism. They may eat only certain foods, and sometimes only certain brands of food. This can be because of taste, texture, smell or some other reason that they are not able to articulate.

People with an autism spectrum condition, including Asperger Syndrome, can be very sensitive to smell, good or bad, such that they can't focus on anything else.

Some children with autism are very sensitive to visual stimuli such as bright lights, colours or things that flicker. It is only too easy to see then how festivals could create a sensory overload for these children. One child notices the small print on posters in the bank and asks the staff about them. However, if asked to go to his room to find his coat or wallet, he will come down without them. When his parents go to look for them, they are usually exactly where they were expected to be, but he has somehow overlooked them!

One more concerning aspect of the sensory differences between neurotypical children and those with autism is that some children with autism either do not feel pain as much as a neurotypical child would, or they are unable to recognize it or let someone know about it. Obviously, this could have serious consequences. One child barely reacted when she broke her wrist, and her parents didn't even take her to the hospital until the next day, yet if her mum so much as taps her to get her attention she yells, 'Ow!'

The above examples show how the senses can be affected by either under- or overstimulation in a child with autism. These effects can happen at any time of day or night and in any situation. Imagine then, how significant they could become at a time of change or transition, such as going on vacation, or at Christmas time or Diwali.

HOW CAN SENSORY OVERLOAD IMPACT ON YOUR CHILD'S BEHAVIOUR?

A sensory overload can have several different effects on your child and how he or she behaves. When everything just gets too much, some children will withdraw into themselves, not talking, appearing not to listen, maybe rocking or showing evidence of tics. Unless you are aware of sensory overload, you may think your child is just being quiet, or even relaxed. Children may freeze in response to a sensory overload, and this can be particularly difficult if you are out in public with them. If your child refuses to move, even you may not understand why, and people around you are likely to stare or even comment. Your child may become visibly distressed, shouting, crying or covering his or her ears. When this happens, hard though it is, try to block out everyone around you, ignore them and just focus on your child. After all, you may never see these people again. They are not important, but your child is.

It can be hard to see the distress your child is feeling. If you can recognize some physical signs in your child that indicate he or she may be starting to experience a sensory overload, such as an increase in tics, then you may be able to teach your child to be aware of these signs. You may have a prearranged sign that your child is able to show you when he or she becomes aware of not 'feeling right'. There may be no typical outward indications, but your child may become snappy or aggressive and this is clearly shown in the example below.

Case study – John

When John and his mum are travelling on the bus, he can't tolerate her talking to him and is very sharp with her if she does. This is probably due to the sensory overload he is experiencing from waiting in the bus queue and having to put up with the noise of traffic and people talking, and often from having been in a shop or other public place before getting on the bus.

John is often very 'short' with her after he has spent time playing with his friends. Even though he has had a good time, he still experiences sensory overload and always takes it out on his mum when the friend has gone. He refuses to accept that he has a sensory overload, and says that the way he is feeling is all her fault. He says things such as, 'If you weren't so stupid, I'd be okay!' or, 'Why are you starting an argument?', if his mum has simply asked him a civil question! It is probably because he thinks his parents will limit the amount of time he spends with his friends if he admits that sometimes they can be overwhelming for him. He will only play with one friend at a time and finds being with more than one friend far too challenging, whether he admits it or not. John can, however, still experience sensory overload when playing with just one friend.

One of the dangers of sensory overload is that, in response to noise, for example, your child may run away to try to escape the source of the noise. This can be particularly dangerous near roads or in unfamiliar places.

Remember, there may or may not be visible signs of sensory overload in your child; or maybe the signs will be different for your child than for a neurotypical child, so it is a case of learning to recognize them – as with John on the bus and playing with his friends. It is impossible to list all the signs of sensory overload, as each child will be different. If at all possible, observe your child, especially at 'risky' times such as a time of change or transition, in a new situation or one that you know your child finds difficult. Observe his or her behaviour, and this may give you some clues on how to minimize the effects of sensory overload in the future.

Just one more point here, which can be highlighted by the following case study:

Case study – Bob

If he experiences a sensory overload, this can affect him for days. He may be snappy or have an emotional outburst the same day, the next day or in the week that follows. This used to be particularly true between Christmas and New Year and after returning from holidays. So, the behaviour that your son or daughter displays today may be as a result of a sensory overload yesterday or even last week! This piece of information may not have been studied or proved, but it is definitely true where Bob is concerned.

REDUCING SENSORY OVERLOAD AND ITS EFFECT ON OUR CHILDREN'S BEHAVIOUR

This will vary for each child, but below are some of the things that parents have tried that have been helpful for their child.

Noise

Earplugs can be helpful for children with auditory sensitivity, especially in noisy places such as the supermarket. Just be aware that if children are going out alone, they will need to be able to hear the sound of traffic and of the people around them for their own safety. Using headphones with an audio book or music CD, or even with some relaxing sounds on, can be very helpful. This can be particularly valuable at airports, train stations and so on.

Try introducing children to noise gradually; gradual exposure coupled with rewards for trying can be very effective. If you know in advance that you are going to a noisy place, or even a place that isn't considered noisy by neurotypical standards, but you know will irritate your child, try talking to your child in advance. It is a good idea to back this up with something visual, such as a script, sign or sketch (see Chapter 9, 'Scripts, Signs and Sketches'). A sign can be very useful, because children can carry this with them and show it to you if they recognize that they are starting to feel unhappy in some way. It may be time consuming to plan ahead with your child who has autism, but it is very worthwhile. Sometimes you may need to remove children from the situation if things are becoming too overwhelming for them.

Touch

If children are sensitive to wearing new clothes, only introduce new items of clothing one at a time. Reward children with praise, or a small reward such as stickers or occasionally chocolate, for taking small steps such as having a new item of clothing in their wardrobe, trying it on or wearing it for a few minutes before changing back into their old favourites. As time goes by, you will probably find that children are more ready to try new clothes as they gain confidence. The same techniques can be applied to wearing sun cream, having their haircut, or taking a bath or shower. Most things can be achieved with time, patience, encouragement and reward. This is far easier to type than it has ever been to do in real life! You will get frustrated with your child's lack of flexibility, and sometimes you may let your frustration show. Don't be too hard on yourself and just keep trying.

It can be very upsetting if, when you desperately want to hug and cuddle your child, he or she won't let you. Here is an example from Bob's life to illustrate this.

Case study – Bob

His dad longs to be physically close to him, but Bob just can't tolerate this. He is very affectionate with his mum and often hugs her, but he finds it impossible to do this with anyone else. He does crave physical contact with his dad, and shows this by playfighting and wrestling with him. He is also able to hug and kiss his dogs, which he does on and off all day! His parents believe it is very important not to force physical affection on to any child, whether or not they have autism. They have a basic human right not to be touched by another person unless they want to be. Bob's parents have never forced, or even encouraged him to, for example, kiss his aunties or grandparents. If he is not comfortable, then he shouldn't have to do it.

This is a difficult area, because if children do allow themselves to be cuddled, they may enjoy it and find it comforting. It will also help them to prepare for more intimate relationships in adulthood. Perhaps you can encourage them to tolerate a small amount of physical contact, such as hand holding, and build on this slowly.

Visual

If children are extremely sensitive to the fluorescent lights in supermarkets, for example, it may be possible for them to wear sunglasses indoors. This may make them somewhat conspicuous, especially if it is not summer. However, if they have an emotional outburst in the supermarket because of sensory overload, they are going to be even more noticeable!

Peak caps are another possibility for providing partial shade. Some children can be very sensitive to colour and other visual stimuli. If this is the case with your child, it may be worth reading the books of people such as Tony Attwood and Philip Whittaker, or books written by people with autism, such as Liane Holliday Willey or Donna Williams. They may be able to offer more substantial advice than we can.

Taste and smell

Sensory issues around taste and smell can cause lots of problems for children with autism. If children will only eat certain foods, or foods with a particular colour or texture, this will lead to anxiety in you because you are worried about their nutrition, and are probably frustrated at having to do separate meals from the rest of the family. Lots of children have this fastidiousness about food, not just children with autism. Letting your anxiety show to the child will only exacerbate the problem. Often, parents can be heard talking about the child's difficulties in front of the child; this reinforces for the child, 'Yes, this is something that I can't do.' It is best to stay calm at meal times and introduce new foods very slowly.

Never try to force new food on the child, and try not to show your dismay when all your attempts fail. This is very hard to do, and you will probably reveal your frustration to the child every now and then. Try not to berate yourself for this; you are a parent trying to do the best for your child. You will make mistakes sometimes – in our case, often!

Just keep going and don't forget to remind yourself what a good parent you actually are. If you weren't, you wouldn't even be reading this book.

It is always a good idea to show our children how much we appreciate the effort that they are making when they try to be flexible. If children allow new food on their plates, but don't eat it, reward them. If they try a tiny bit and spit it out, reward them. Reward can be praise or an actual small reward. It is more important to reward children's efforts than their success. Success is often a reward in itself, but if children try and don't succeed, then their self-esteem may be affected, so always let them know how much you respect their efforts. It can be a good idea to put new food on a separate plate; this way it can be moved away quickly if necessary, and it is not so threatening for children as it might be if it were sitting on their plate challenging them!

Olfactory sensitivity can work both ways, as with other senses we have discussed above, and a person can be hyper- or hyposensitive to smell. Some children with autism can smell 'too well'; they are hypersensitive to smell, which can often be so overpowering for them that they can only focus on that smell and are unable to focus on anything else. This can obviously cause problems; for example, at school. Also, the child may feel a need to get away from the smell but may not be able to articulate this and so could display what the parent may think of as challenging behaviour, but is really just a desperate attempt to escape something that is overwhelmingly unpleasant for that child. A person who is affected by an autism-related condition may be opposed to smells that would not bother, or not even be detected by, a neurotypical person! If a person smells the odour of a food they don't like, this can cause them to lose their appetite and so render them unable to eat the food they do like. Again, if they cannot express this then it is possible their reaction will be seen as 'fussy eating' or wilfulness when it is in fact nothing of the sort.

Parents of children with autism can often be heard talking about the fact that their children sniff and smell things that neurotypical people probably wouldn't feel the need to smell, such as objects and other people! It is possible that children get some pleasure from this if they like the smell, or maybe it is their way of familiarizing themselves with their surroundings to give themselves a sense of comfort and reassurance.

Our son often used to comment on the smell of people when he was younger, saying that each person had their own smell, not necessarily unpleasant, just distinct – for example, he often said his dad smelled of leather!

It is also possible that the person with autism may not be offended by smells that most neurotypical people would find offensive.

TECHNIQUES TO HELP AVOID SENSORY OVERLOAD

If you can anticipate a sensory overload, for example, a trip to the supermarket, visitors to the house, festival times or vacations, then you can try to prepare your child for it. The transition techniques we use for particular times of the day, week, year and so on are described in detail in later chapters in this book. Below are some additional techniques you may like to try as well.

- Talk to your child beforehand about the situation you are going to be in and how he or she might be affected by it. Use your judgement here, because, sometimes, talking to a child too much can create more anxiety.

- Use signs, sketches and scripts to help your child to learn about the situation, about the emotions this may evoke and how these emotions may impact on his or her behaviour (see Chapter 9, 'Scripts, Signs and Sketches').

- If you know in advance which situation is likely to create a sensory overload for your child, try to introduce it gradually; for example, you could go on a bus at a quiet time of day. This may need to be built up very slowly by first just walking past a bus stop on the opposite side of the road; then past the bus stop itself; waiting at the stop but not actually getting on the bus; getting on the bus for one stop only, and so on. As always, give lots of praise for any effort made by your child.

- Give your child a comfort item if appropriate. This may be a book or favourite toy, or some other item which your child is attached to. This will give your child something positive to focus on.

- If your child has a special interest, try using this and integrating it into the situation. For example, if your child loves dinosaurs then you can take one with you, and perhaps make up a story about a dinosaur in that particular situation (although a child with Asperger Syndrome is likely to correct you and remind you that a dinosaur couldn't go to a train station because they became extinct 60 million years ago!). You could just bring along a book about the special interest, or talk about it a lot. You may be able to point out something that is related to the specialized subject. This will focus your child's mind so he isn't so agitated by the sights and sounds around him.

- Distraction techniques can be useful with all children. We have found that our son enjoys making lists (e.g., top ten films, books, etc.), and this helps to keep him focused and often keeps sensory overload at bay. If you are able to distract your child before the situation gets out of hand, you may have some success in preventing or minimizing a sensory overload and the consequences of this.

- With time and patience, you may be able to get your child to use some kind of 'scale' to indicate his or her stress levels to you, such as a picture of a thermometer or a ladder, where the greater the feelings of stress, the higher up the ladder or thermometer he or she would point. This may not be possible if your child is already too anxious and wound up.

WHEN SENSORY OVERLOAD IS UNEXPECTED

If you can't anticipate a sensory overload but it happens anyway, the most important thing is to keep you and your child safe. Try not to worry too much about what the people around you are thinking. This is very hard to do, especially if your child is telling you to shut up and calling you stupid by this point! It is a worry that, as your child gets bigger, someone may try to get involved or call the police. It is up to you and your child whether or not to tell people that the child has autism, and that actually it would be more helpful if they just left you alone to deal with your child. Some children may not want the people around them to know about their autism. The National Autistic Society has little cards that parents or people with autism can hand out to members of the public for situations like this; that way you don't have to spend time explaining when your attention obviously needs to be focused on your child in that moment. These cards can be very helpful, but your child's privacy and self-esteem also has to be considered, so talk to your child in advance about the idea of using these cards in public.

If possible, it can be a good idea to ignore the negative behaviour until you and your child are home and safe, and deal with it then. This isn't letting your child get away with negative behaviour; it just helps to prevent the situation from becoming any more explosive than it has to be. Letting things go at the time and waiting until a more appropriate time to deal with them is very, very hard to do. This is especially hard if your child is coming across as loud, rude or even aggressive towards you in public. It can feel very humiliating, and have a negative effect on your own self-esteem, but the alternative – a full-blown outburst or meltdown in public – should be avoided wherever possible.

When your child's stress levels rise, it is highly likely that yours will, too! It is tempting, to say the least, to raise your own voice or to speak very quickly, issuing demands or threats, or just vocalizing how stressed you are feeling in that moment. This will only add to your child's sensory overload and inflame the situation, so try to avoid it wherever possible.

There is more advice later in the book on dealing with sensory overload, especially for the times when you are out and about with your child and he or she is becoming agitated or even aggressive because of it (see Chapter 9, 'Scripts, Signs and Sketches'.)

We believe that sensory overload is often the trigger behind a child's outbursts, but sometimes the signs are so hard to spot that you often can't catch it in time!

At times of change and transition, your child is likely to experience a sensory overload at some point. Later on in the book we talk about some of these times of transition and change and how you can help your child to deal with them calmly in order to avoid, or at least minimize, sensory overload and the fallout from this.

Bob's comments

An example of a sensory overload could be last week, when Dad changed our plans at short notice and we ended up going shopping to the Trafford Centre at about 12.30 pm, rather than 6 pm. This meant that my plans for the afternoon were completely changed, and it also happens to be the busiest time of day at the Trafford Centre. We argued a bit with each other when we were there, and I was finding it really hard to make a decision about which shoes to buy, but we got some in the end and went home. My plans were changed again at short notice the next morning, when Mum decided she was too ill to go to the gym, but needed me to go food shopping with her. When we got back, I was carrying all the heavy bags and Mum had nothing in her hands, and she walked directly past the kitchen door without opening it and went into the lounge to blow her nose. That left me trying to close the front door while carrying all the heavy shopping bags, without being able to get into the kitchen. This annoyed me, but what started the argument was that Mum couldn't see that she'd done anything wrong. She tried to say it was my fault for not putting the shopping down and opening the door myself. One thing led to another, and we ended up having a full-blown argument with each other. I don't think our reactions or the arguing would have been as extreme if it hadn't been for the big changes in my plans that day and the day before. I was still annoyed at Dad from the day before, as it meant I couldn't do what I had planned for the afternoon and there was absolutely no reason for it at all. If we had gone at 6 pm it would have been a lot quieter and with fewer crowds than there were at lunch time. Also, I was planning to watch a film in the morning while Mum was at the gym and then go shopping, but I wasn't able to do this as Mum was too ill for the gym. So this is both an example of sensory overload and of changes at short notice that to some people might seem small, but to some of us can have a very big effect.

A lot of the time you might not recognize that you are having a sensory overload. This is why hindsight is so important – being able to look back and see that you have had a sensory overload, and work out what you can do to prevent it next time. If people with autism aren't able to able to do this for themselves, then it is the parent's responsibility to do this for them, for everyone's sake.

PART TWO

---- · · · ·

EXAMPLES OF TIMES OF CHANGE AND HOW TO USE THE TRANSITION TECHNIQUES AT THESE TIMES

5
WEEKENDS

He has no idea on weekends or holidays…which causes no end of problems…

(Mother of Oliver, aged 5)

The change from weekday to weekend mode and back again occurs so often that most of us take it for granted. We don't always like it, and many of us get that sinking 'Monday morning' feeling when it comes to going back to work or school, at the thought of having to get up early and face the coming week. We would rather have more time off, and more time to ourselves to do the things we enjoy, and to choose how we spend our time instead of having to study or earn a living, even if we enjoy our job or our study. If you are a person with autism it is likely that you will be even more sensitive to these changes and feel them more acutely. It won't necessarily be about wanting the weekend to continue as much as being anxious about a forthcoming change. In fact, people with autism may be just as anxious about the change from Friday into Saturday as they are about the change from Sunday to Monday. At the very least they will feel apprehensive, but possibly even fearful of having to face what to them feels like an enormous amount of change.

If you actually think about it, a lot of change takes place when you go from weekday to weekend mode and back again. Many parents notice that these seemingly minor changes cause a lot of anxiety for their children, especially the change from the more relaxed atmosphere of Saturday and Sunday to the more organized routine of Monday. This can work in reverse for some people with autism, who cope better with the structure of the week and are more anxious about the 'freedom' that the weekend can bring. If you have a child with autism you may have noticed that your child displays 'difficult' behaviour either as the week or the weekend draw to a close, and it may not be apparent to you, or to your son or daughter, why this is the case. As discussed in the chapter on emotions, such children may be unable to recognize what they are feeling, and even if they have some inkling of why they are feeling as they are, they may not be able to articulate this to you if they struggle with the expression of their emotions.

The following case study illustrates just how confusing and distressing the changes around weeks and weekends can be, and the negative effect these can have on our children's behaviour.

Case study – Bob

Monday mornings have always been problematic for Bob and his family. While he tended to have big emotional outbursts on most days, the build-up to these wasn't always obvious, and his parents couldn't see them coming. However, this was never true of Monday mornings! They could predict in advance that he would be snappy, and eventually distressed and even aggressive on Monday mornings. Meltdowns are hard to prevent when you can't see them coming (especially as so many people with autism don't show their emotions in their facial expressions); but Monday mornings presented Bob's parents with a good opportunity to head off one of his outbursts. It was the perfect time to use the transition techniques to explain to Bob that the weekend was over and that things would be different, and the pace of life would change on Monday morning. It was much easier for Bob to understand and absorb this information when his parents drew pictures and made notes or sketches about the weekend and the weekdays, illustrating what the similarities and differences were likely to be. Bob was always able to understand this information intellectually, but it was the effect it had on his emotions that created the difficulties. Just taking some time to write and draw about these changes allowed Bob to think things through at his own pace, to know what to expect and so be able to prepare for the weekend–weekday transition with more confidence and certainty.

Bob is home educated, so this may have been easier for us than it would be for a family whose child goes to school, but the techniques used can still be helpful (see later on in this chapter and further chapters for examples of techniques). In this situation, you can use the transition techniques on Sunday evening when your child may be more relaxed and better able to absorb what you are telling him or her. It may even help to ward off any anxiety and concern about the following day that your child may be feeling at bedtime. Everyone feels anxious if they are not sure what to expect and our children are no different. Working with them around the changes from weekend to weekday mode and back again should help to reduce this anxiety and make life that bit easier for the whole family.

USING THE TRANSITION TECHNIQUES

Preparation is all important; our transition techniques are all about preparing your child intellectually and emotionally to deal with change.

Talking to your child on Friday and doing some visual work about the changes that the weekend will bring will help convey this information in a friendly and non-threatening way. It may take a while to get used to using these techniques, and your child may not want to join in to begin with, but if you do the writing and drawing and just let your child watch, he or she may eventually want to take part. Even without active involvement, your child will still be absorbing the information. It is reassuring for your child just to be alerted to the upcoming changes, and to recognize that you are aware of any difficulties. The transition techniques may not eliminate all feelings of fear and anxiety, but they should help your child to achieve some sense of control in the face of the negative and confusing feelings that he or she may be experiencing. It is a good idea to talk about any of these feelings that your child may be experiencing. As children with autism often find it hard to express and read feelings this may be something you do separately, to help in all areas of your child's life and refer to regularly at times such as weekends (see Chapter 3, 'Emotions').

These transition techniques will only take a few minutes out of your day. They won't work miracles but they should help to relieve some of the stress and anxiety that may be building up in your child. They have certainly helped us.

Following is a description of the techniques we developed to use with our child to help him to cope with the change from weekday to weekend mode and back again.

If your child wants to, involve him or her in writing or drawing.

You can use photographs or pictures from magazines if you or your child prefer this to drawing.

On Friday evening:

- Write a list, using paper and pens/pencils/felt tips/crayons, etc. of the things you have done during the week. For us, this would involve things around home education, friends coming to play, dog training and so on. For you, this may involve school, social activities and so on. It is a way of going over the week and drawing it to a close.

- Talk (or write or draw) about the forthcoming weekend: the things you will be doing, what to expect, and what will be different about the weekend to the weekdays.

On Sunday evening:

- Talk with your child about how the weekend has gone. What did you do? What did your child enjoy or not enjoy?

- Talk to your child about the forthcoming week and anything that will be coming up that week; for example, an appointment or a social visit. We talked to our son about his home education, explaining that it will be starting again on Monday morning.

- Write a weekly plan so that your child knows roughly what to expect each day, and keep this in a place where he or she can easily refer to it.

On Monday morning:

- We usually took things easy regarding our son's home education to ease him gently back into it. If your child goes to school you may not be able to do this, but you could talk with your child's teacher about the difficulties the change from weekend to weekday can cause for your child, and see if you can come to some arrangement with the school.

  Note: lots of children with an autism spectrum condition attend mainstream schools, but often teaching staff are not given the training they need to make sense of our children's behaviour. This is unfair on the staff and on our children. If your child does attend a mainstream school, don't be afraid to educate the teaching staff about autism and how it affects your child – they may be the education experts, but you are the expert on your child. You will probably find that they are glad of your help and support, as they may be feeling out of their depth if they are not experienced in the area of autism spectrum condition. You will also be helping to pave the way for children with autism who come along after your child has grown and moved on.

You can also use these techniques each evening to help your child cope with the transition of one day going into another. Talk to your child and use pen and paper to illustrate points that you want to emphasize. Ask them about the day and go over what will be happening the next day. Pictures and signs can be really useful here. For some children, a discussion about what to expect in the entire week ahead may just be too overwhelming, and you may need to take things one day at a time. Alternatively, you may talk about the week ahead but still do the transition techniques from day to day as well. Only you will know what suits your child – or you may find that you learn this by trial and error!

It is very much up to you as a family to decide how much writing and talking to do. Some children may prefer this to be kept to a minimum, and concentrate more on the drawings (see Chapter 9, 'Scripts, Signs and Sketches'). Your attempt at these transition techniques may be hit and miss at first, but as you will see from the examples that follow, the techniques are very basic. The drawings are all stick figures, so you don't need to be skilled at drawing or writing to do these techniques; and as we mentioned earlier, children may want to do the drawings themselves. After a few attempts you should feel more confident with using these techniques.

We created the transition techniques in a way that suited our son, but you may prefer to change them into whatever format is best for you and your child. Please use them as a guide, but experiment with them as much as you like – we really want you to have some success with them in any way that is best for your family.

Case study – Robert

The beginning of the week was always difficult for Robert and his family. He would often have outbursts, shouting and crying, completely unable to cope with the changes taking place as Sunday turned into Monday, and the weekend routine ended and weekday routine began.

His parents spent some time on Sunday afternoon and evening talking to Robert about the changes that would take place as the new week began. They explained to him that the weekend was over, and that things would be different on Monday morning. His mum talked to him about all the things they had done over the weekend and they drew pictures about it. Next, they spoke about the things that would be happening on Monday and in particular, what would be different. They went back through the pictures they had drawn for Sunday and crossed out all of the pictures that wouldn't be relevant for Monday; for example, getting up late, visiting grandparents and going swimming. Mum and Robert then talked about the things that would be happening instead on Monday, and drew pictures about that; for example, school, chess-club and early bedtime.

This helped him to understand that a change would be taking place and what this change would be. It helped to relieve some of the confusion and anxiety that Robert had been experiencing up to that point.

His parents continued to use these transition techniques every Friday and Sunday. Robert still struggles with change. He may always struggle, but he has made very good progress, and is certainly more confident about dealing with the change from weekday to weekend mode and back again. His parents are now at the point where they believe that he doesn't always need to go through these transition techniques unless he is showing particular signs of anxiety.

TO SUM UP

- On Fridays, write and draw about the difference between weekdays and weekends.

- Do the same on Sunday evenings, but in reverse.

- The same techniques can also help your child to cope with the change of one day going into another.

- You may find that you only need to use these techniques for a while, until your child gets more used to the changes that take place during the transition period from weekday to weekend mode or vice versa or it may be that the use of the techniques is an ongoing activity for you and your child.

- Remember, preparation can mean the difference between a distressed child and a reasonably confident child.

- You can use photographs or pictures from magazines if you prefer not to draw.

- All of the above may sound like a lot of work, but it will only take a few minutes and you and your child may find it very helpful in the short and long term.

Please look at the examples at the end of the chapter, to help you to make more sense of the techniques that are described above.

Bob's comments

Weekends were obviously a difficulty for quite a while, so the transition techniques really helped. Monday mornings are difficult for anyone, but if you find it hard coping with change they are probably ten times as difficult. Even good changes can be confusing and difficult, and they are even harder to change back from. The techniques don't work instantly and will take a while to get going, but they are well worth doing. Even though it may take a few weeks or months to get used to using the techniques, it is hoped you will get to a point where you no longer need to use them at all, so it will have been well worth taking the time to put them into practice in the first place. I reached this point several years ago and now don't even think about the change from week to weekend, except to look forward to it as a break from college. So I have gone from viewing weekends as a bad thing because of the uncertainty of the changes involved, to enjoying them and not even thinking about the change. The techniques might not get everybody to this point and you may always need to use them to help to get you through the changes involved in the weekends, but even if you do not get to this point, at least they will make the weekends easier for you and serve as a reminder to the non-autistic people in your family of how challenging change can be.

Friday pm example

How did this week go for Bob?

Bob did his home education from Monday to Friday.

On Tuesday evening Philip came to play.

On Wednesday morning Casey came to play and on Thursday evening Bob and Mum went to Joseph's house.

Bob went swimming with Mum on Tuesday and Thursday morning.

On Tuesday night Bob went to dog training and on Wednesday night Bob went to the gym.

It has been another busy week and now it's time to wind down a bit for the weekend.

We will still do lots of things over the weekend but Bob can go to bed later and get up later. He can also have some time to sit around watching TV, or reading if he wants to.

Figure 5.1: Transition technique: Friday pm. How did this week go for Bob?

Friday pm examples continued

What plans do we have for the weekend?

 No home education except maths with Kate on Saturday morning at 9 am until 10 am.

 Go to bed half an hour later.

 I am going to the cinema on Saturday with Dad at 2.30 pm.

 Mum, Dad and I will take the dogs for a run on the river banks, if the weather is nice enough. We will probably do this on Sunday afternoon.

Poppy and Fred

 I may go to the gym with Mum and Dad at about 11 am on Sunday.

Bob on the treadmill

Figure 5.2: Transition technique: Friday pm. What plans do we have for the weekend?

Sunday pm example

How was the weekend?

- What did you enjoy about the weekend?

> I enjoyed going to the cinema, eating chocolate and taking the dogs out.

- Was there anything you didn't enjoy?

> Maths!

> The gym was okay.

- Tomorrow is Monday, the start of a new week. You will start your work again but first we can go into town to look around the charity shops. You will need to get up by 7.30 am and be in bed by 9.30 pm.

> We have another busy week planned. It goes roughly as follows but you can check the calendar each night to see what is happening the next day.

Figure 5.3: Transition technique: Sunday pm. How was the weekend?

Weekly plan - remember this may change

	Morning	Afternoon	Evening
Monday -	Charity shops	Re-start home education	Relax
Tuesday -	Swimming H.E.	H.E. Philip 3.30 pm	Dog training
Wednesday -	H.E.	H.E. Casey 1 pm	Gym with Mum
Thursday -	Swimming H.E.	H.E.	Joseph's 5.30 pm
Friday -	Grandparents	H.E.	Relax with Dad

- What are you looking forward to next week?
    Swimming, seeing friends.

- Is there anything you are not looking forward to?
    Maths, spellings.

Figure 5.4: Weekly plan

6
VACATIONS
AND HOLIDAYS

When we go on holiday everything changes. Even a weekend away throws up major changes. Even though he loves holidays, he still gets very anxious about the change of routine and this can affect his behaviour...

(Father of Bob, aged 16)

We all look forward to vacations and benefit from them in the long run, but they can be stressful, even for neurotypical people. All the planning and organizing and the change from routine can be fun but also a bit daunting and overwhelming, particularly for people with autism.

Vacations offer a complete change – of environment, weather, culture, food, currency, language, and also a break from school or work, and a lot more time spent with the people you are travelling with. And when you return from vacation, there is the transition back to everyday life mode. No wonder vacations can be so stressful for our families!

TRAVELLING
However you choose to travel when you go on vacation, there will be some level of change. This may mean being in the car when you wouldn't normally be, or for longer periods than normal. Travel by coach, train or plane is probably not something your child would do every day or even regularly.

There will also be increased contact with other people: airport or railway staff, other passengers, other customers in busy motorway cafes and so on. There will be different noises, sights, sounds and smells, and your child will have to cope with all of these. This could lead to a sensory overload, and this is something you need to be aware of, and possibly plan for (see Chapter 4, 'Sensory Overload').

Case study – Bob

When travelling, his family try to prepare Bob in advance by keeping a record book about their travels. Before their journey begins, they write down what will happen on the day that they travel: what time they will get up, what time they will leave the house, which methods of transport they will use (e.g., a taxi to the airport and then an aeroplane), what will happen at the airport, what will happen on the plane, and what will happen when they arrive at their destination.

This preparation and planning really helps to prepare Bob emotionally for the forthcoming changes. There is such a big transition to go through, and talking, writing and drawing about these changes give him more chance of understanding and absorbing the information his parents are trying to convey. He seems more accepting of the changes and has a calmer approach to them.

It is always a good idea for you or your child to draw pictures when explaining things to him or her. This makes things more relaxed and less formal, and also helps to convey the information more effectively. It is often said that people with autism learn visually, so using pictures, photographs, sketches and so on will in all probability be very helpful.

Talking about each event as it is coming up will go some way to preparing your child. It is helpful, in addition, to carry pictures, signs that your child can use to tell you if he or she is becoming overwhelmed or anxious, and signs that you can use to remind your child about what is coming up next (e.g., a picture of an aeroplane). If you have done some work with your child in advance of the travelling, then going over scripts, signs or sketches that you may have prepared in advance should help to keep your child calm by acting as a reminder of the things you have already discussed (see Chapter 9, 'Scripts, Signs and Sketches' for more detailed information).

Examples of scripts that can be used when travelling
Aeroplane

- We will walk up some steps to board the plane.

- The cabin crew will say hello to us and tell us where to sit.

- We will wear seatbelts.

- There will be lots of other passengers.

- The cabin crew will walk up and down the aisle serving drinks and snacks.

- We can use the toilets but there may be a queue.

- The captain will tell us when it is time to land.

- We will stay in our seats until most of the other people have left the plane, then we will get off and go into the airport.

Train

- We will sit together on the train.

- We may be able to buy drinks and snacks from the bar or from someone walking down the aisle selling them.

- There will be toilets but we may have to queue.

- Someone may come to check our tickets.

- We will look at the names of the stations as we pass by and get off the train when we see our station.

Taxi

- Mum or Dad will phone to order a taxi.

- The taxi will come to our house.

- We will sit in the back.

- We will wear seatbelts.

- When we arrive at our destination Mum or Dad will pay the taxi driver and we will get out of the taxi.

These scripts are very basic and just meant as examples. It is always best to personalize scripts so that they make more sense to individual children; for example, you may want to say who they will be sitting next to on the train, or if they will be bringing their favourite toy on to the plane.

The way you write the script may depend on the age and level of understanding of your child. Use language that you feel is appropriate, and always try to keep scripts short and simple. It can be tempting to write a lot because there is so much you want your child to understand, but it is quite well documented that no matter how intelligent your child with autism is, it can take longer for information to be processed. Never give too many instructions in one go, or too much information too quickly – this can lead to a sensory overload and create more problems than it solves (see Chapter 4, 'Sensory Overload').

You may want to make scripts and signs that talk about the places you will be going to get on to the transport, such as train stations and airports. Draw pictures, cut pictures out of magazines or use the internet to illustrate the points you are trying to make, and to show your child images of the train station or airport, for example. Spend time with your child going over the scripts before you visit these places to help him or her become familiar with what to expect.

It is a good idea to put these scripts or signs on to manageable size cards and laminate them so you can carry them with you on your journey. You may find that your child feels less anxious by just holding the script or sign as a reminder of what is going to happen. This has been our experience; our son used to get comfort from simply holding a sign that we had designed to help him to cope with change. Sometimes we would not even have to talk it through with him; he would just hold on to it and it must have reminded him about the work we had already done with him. An example of this is a sign he used to hold to remind him not to shout, as this upset the dogs. The sign featured a drawing of the dogs, and the message, 'Let's calm down so we don't upset the dogs'. We would give it him to hold at times when we knew his anxiety levels would be rising, potentially leading to an outburst (such as when he was attempting to do writing and spelling, which he finds extremely frustrating because of his dyslexia and dyspraxia). When travelling, he often found it helpful to hold a laminated list of our itinerary.

Examples of signs that can be used when travelling

Figure 6.1: Aeroplane

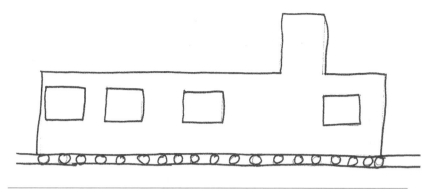

Figure 6.2: Train

Figure 6.3: Taxi

CHANGE OF BEDTIME AND GETTING-UP TIME

This can be very disruptive for your child. Often, when going on vacation, people have to get up particularly early to prepare for a long drive or to catch a flight. Many parents find that any change in bedtime routine can cause major problems for their children, especially if the child has autism. Children with autism often have sleep problems anyway, and so a disruption of their bedtime can be very unsettling.

If you add this to all the other changes that vacations bring, it is no wonder our children may become distressed, confused and display challenging behaviour at this time.

Case study – Bob

When preparing for a vacation, Bob's parents write down what time he will be going to bed and getting up, and how this might affect him. An example of this would be something like, 'You will be getting up two hours early, at 5 am. You may feel tired because of this.' Bob's parents have found that this helps to calm their son because he then knows what to expect. Before they started trying to prepare him for a forthcoming vacation, they observed that Bob would get very anxious in the days preceding the trip and this would be displayed in his behaviour, causing significant upset for the whole family. He would also get very distressed on return from the vacation, and continue to be so for up to two weeks afterwards. Since the techniques have been implemented to help their son to deal with these times of change, going on vacation has been a much more positive experience for the whole family.

Even sleeping in a different bed, which can feel strange for anyone, can feel quite threatening for a child with autism; the feel, the smell and everything about it is different from what the child is used to at home. If possible, take along the child's usual bedding, or even just the pillow. For some children, it may be enough to take the toy that they normally sleep with, as you might for neurotypical children; however, your child with autism may need some additional support to sleep happily in a different bed. This is another situation where it can be useful to write a script or make a sign or sketch in advance of the occasion. Keep the information simple, explaining any differences or similarities that your child can expect and for how long. Pitch the information at your child's level of understanding. Try to be aware of any sensory problems that your child may be experiencing in the different bed: smell, texture of bedding, temperature, colours and so on. A little bit of forethought and preparation could ward off any anxiety your child may experience, and enable him or her to settle into the new routine and feel secure.

Children are often allowed to stay up late when they are on vacation, which can ultimately lead to overexcitement and tiredness. It is tempting to say that you should stick to your child's usual bedtime routine when on vacation, but this would probably be too difficult to carry through, and anyway, it is good for our children to experience change and learn to be flexible. The trick is to learn how to do this with the minimum level of disruption and upset. It can help just to be aware that a change in bedtime routine may affect your child's behaviour, and thus be emotionally prepared for it. By using the transition techniques we describe in this book, you will be able to prepare for and deal with some of the anxiety and distress caused by these changes. If your child's sleep is disrupted when you are away on holiday, there will be an effect on his or her behaviour during the vacation, and also for some weeks after returning home. And obviously, if your child isn't sleeping then you are unlikely to sleep and this will have an impact on the enjoyment of your vacation. If you can help your child with any sleep issues on vacation, the experience of being away will be a much more positive one for everyone concerned.

CHANGE OF ENVIRONMENT

When you go on vacation everything changes, whether you are going abroad or just to a seaside resort half an hour's drive up the motorway. The scenery, the surroundings, the climate, the place you will be calling home for the duration of your stay – all this and more is different. While many neurotypical people look forward to and are excited about getting away from their routine and experiencing a new environment (a change is as good as a rest!), people with autism may find these same things daunting and anxiety provoking. The thought of being away from the familiarity of the home environment can be terrifying.

Good preparation may help here. Use strategies and techniques to prepare your child for the change, explaining what will be happening, and what the child can expect. This should help your child to be more accepting of the imminent changes. As well as working with him or her before the vacation, be sure to do some work both while on vacation, and on the return home.

Below are some examples of the change of environment your child will experience when going on vacation:

- The external environment – the area surrounding your child that you may be exploring on your vacation. Most children love the countryside or the seaside but for a child who has an autism spectrum condition, even such an exciting and stimulating environment may create lots of anxieties in the child. This change may just be too much for them and could lead to a sensory overload and cause the child to present with challenging behaviour or to become very withdrawn. As we discuss many times in this book, even a small change can be distressing, but a vacation usually entails a complete change of environment, which is a massive deal for someone who has autism. At a time when you expect your child to be happy and relaxed this change in environment may cause resistance in your child, confusion and anxiety. Such a huge change in environment may be just too traumatic for the individual with autism.

Case study – Bob

As Bob has grown and developed, his love of vacations has become more and more apparent; however, it wasn't always this way. Being in a completely different environment used to throw Bob into a complete state of panic and had an inevitable effect on his behaviour. One of the ways his parents dealt with this was to return to the same vacation destination every year. His dad's friend has an apartment in Ibiza and so Bob and his parents were able to return to the same location, same apartment, same restaurants, same beaches and so on, year after year. Strangely enough this actually helped Bob to become more flexible when it came to going on vacation to other places in later years, as his parents were able to use Ibiza as a positive example of somewhere Bob had never been that ended up being a home from home!

- Change of the internal environment – the place the family stays when on vacation. This is obviously going to be a complete change of environment than the child`s actual home. Using the transition techniques, you can talk these changes through with your child. Do this at your child's pace to avoid creating further anxiety. Each child will be different and have different levels of understanding and different levels of anxiety, so use your knowledge of your own son or daughter to gauge how to present this information.

  Children who have autism often benefit from time alone in a safe place, such as their bedroom. In a vacation environment this may not be possible and even if the child does have their own room to stay in, that room won't be familiar. It may help to bring some of the child's favourite belongings to make the room more friendly and try to ensure that the child has some alone time after a busy day on the beach, for example, if your child is someone who needs time by him- or herself after social contact or sensory bombardment.

- Change of faces – the people surrounding your child will be different on vacation from at home. your child will obviously have some familiar faces with him or her, but will not see the usual people he or she would probably see on a daily basis in his or her own neighbourhood such as friends, extended family, shopkeepers, teachers and so on. It may seem obvious to us that these faces will change, but to our children with autism this may be confusing and distressing. Using transition techniques should help you to explain these forthcoming changes to your child and hopefully help to alleviate some of the anxiety he or she may experience.

Here is an example of a script that may be helpful when trying to explain some of these changes in environment to your child:

Different faces - the script

At home we see people we know each day.

On weekdays we see the teacher and friends from school.

On Tuesday evenings we see Grandma and Granddad.

When we go shopping we often see shopkeepers that we recognize.

When we go on vacation we will not see the people we know.

We will see other people who are on vacation like us.

We will see people who live and work in that place.

The people who serve us in the shops will be different.

It is okay to see people we don't normally see.

These people will probably be nice to us and we will probably like them.

When we return home we will see the people we normally see.

(September 2005)

It is a good idea to personalize the script to make it more accessible to your child. Scripts like this can be used to help explain each change of environment that your child may be facing, and you can also use sketches and signs as explained in Chapter 9, 'Scripts, Signs and Sketches'. Taking photographs with you of your child's home, friends, etc. may be helpful. Also, showing your child photographs, a brochure or an internet site of the place you are going on vacation may help them to become more familiar with the place before you go.

Always take any anxieties your child has regarding going on vacation very seriously, however trivial they may seem to you, and show that you are doing your best to help him or her to deal with these anxieties. For our son the biggest anxiety was the animals – he hated being parted from them and so was involved in making sure they were safe and well cared for while we were away by coming with us to choose kennels, etc. and taking the dogs into kennels when the time came. It also helped him to deal with his own anxieties by reassuring the pets that they would be okay in their new environment for a while and that things would go back to normal when they returned home, just like they would for our son!

Transition techniques to prepare Bob for a vacation and the return home

Please note: the amount of detail in your writing and drawings will depend on the age and level of understanding of your child, so you will need to adapt these accordingly.

- We write a list of questions such as, 'What am I looking forward to when I go on vacation?' or, 'What will I miss about home when I am on vacation?' (The answer to this question is always, 'The dogs!')

- A day or so before we come home from vacation, we go through these techniques again, but in reverse, for example, 'What will I miss most about being on vacation?' or, 'What am I most looking forward to about going home?' (Again, the answer here is always, 'The dogs!')

We go through these questions with our son and he answers them, sometimes drawing pictures at the side (see Figures 6.4; 6.5).

Examples of the holiday diary/record book

Ibiza 2004

We are going to Ibiza on Sunday 12th September.

Before we go Mum and Bob will take the guinea pigs to their hotel!

On Sunday 12th Dad and Bob will take Fred for a long walk before taking him to his hotel!

We will get a taxi to the airport.

Our flight is at 2.50 pm.

Before getting our flight we will look for a story tape for Bob in the airport shop.

- What am I looking forward to about the holiday?

> Swimming, playing on the beach, eating meals out.

- What am I looking forward to eating when I'm in Ibiza?

> Cakes, pastries.

- What will I miss about home when I am in Ibiza?

> The animals.

- How long am I going to Ibiza for?

> One week.

Figure 6.4: Holiday diary/record book: Ibiza 2004

Ibiza 2004 continued

We have been in Ibiza now for five days.

We will be going home on Sunday.

We will get a taxi to the airport.

Our flight is at 3 pm.

- What am I enjoying about being in Ibiza?
Swimming, eating out, the waves, staying up late. ☺

- Am I missing anything about being at home?
Just the animals.

- Is there anything I don't like about being in Ibiza?
Sun cream!

- What am I looking forward to most about going home?
Seeing Fred!

- What am I not looking forward to about going home?
Home education, earlier bedtimes! ☹

Figure 6.5: Holiday diary/record book: Ibiza 2004

We also find it useful to keep a holiday diary while we are away. This is both fun, and a way of helping to reduce our son's anxiety levels. Each day, if possible, we do a little writing and drawing about what we are doing on holiday (see Figure 6.6).

Monday 11th September 2004

I went for a walk to the beach with Dad while Mum snored!

Mum, Dad and I swam in the pool and I practised diving.

We saw some geckos.

We went on the mini-train to a very old church and a very old farm.

We learned about the making of olive oil and saw fig trees, olive trees, carob trees and cacti growing prickly pears.

The last stop was a beach where we had a quick swim.

In the evening we went out for a meal to the same place we went last night – our favourite one in Ibiza.

 The dog we met on the old farm. We think she was called 'Corda'. She was a miniature Yorkshire Terrier.

Figure 6.6: Diary extract: holiday in Ibiza 2006

Alongside this, we do transition techniques similar to those we use to prepare for the changes at Christmas and New Year, and those that take place during the weekday to weekend transition:

- We have a sheet of paper and some felt tip pens. We talk to our son about how things are now, what we do in our day-to-day life. We write these points down and he draws pictures (see Figure 6.7).

Figure 6.7: Transition technique: what life is like on holiday

Before we return from vacation, we do the same process about returning to everyday life from vacation mode (see Figure 6.8).

On our return home, we repeat the above process, talking to Bob about how things are now that we are back at home (see Figure 6.9).

Ibiza 2004 continued

Everyday life → holiday life → everyday life
Transition techniques

Home education.

Bed at 9.30 pm.

Being with the pets.

Swimming twice a week.

Everyday life

Chocolate twice a week.

Probably lots of rain.

Figure 6.8: Transition technique: return to everyday life: Ibiza 2004

Tuesday 21st September 2004

Now I am home from Ibiza!

- How do I feel now I am home from Ibiza?

  Glad to be back but upset that I am no longer in Ibiza!

- What do I miss most about Ibiza?

  Beach, pool, swimming, waves, sun, sea, geckos, cakes and pastries.

- What is the best thing about being home?

  The animals!

- Was Fred pleased to see me?

  Yes!

Bob   Fred

Figure 6.9: Holiday diary/record book: Ibiza 2004

As Bob is allowed to stay up late on vacation, we gradually bring his bedtime back to the normal time. We also decide which day he will restart his home education and record how we will build up to this, starting with a small amount of work and aiming to get back to normal after about a week (before we began using these transition techniques, this used to take at least two weeks).

During this time of change and transition, we use the reward plan we developed to support our son with the more challenging aspects of his Asperger Syndrome (see our first book, *Create a Reward Plan for Your Child with Asperger Syndrome* for details).

HOW TRANSITION TECHNIQUES HAVE WORKED FOR US

Our transition techniques have significantly reduced the problems we experience as a family when dealing with the stress and anxiety that vacations create. Our son is so much more confident about going on vacation and travelling all together now. The biggest improvements are in the reduced amount of time it now takes us to get him settled back into his bedtime routine and his home education routine. But most particularly, the number and intensity of emotional outbursts he has before, during, and especially after, a vacation are significantly reduced.

At the time of writing this, our son has gone camping with his dad and he has shown no signs of anxiety in the build-up to this vacation. In the past, he would have been incredibly anxious, constantly asking questions and worrying about the forthcoming change. He would have been worried about all the things that might go wrong on the vacation, so much so that it would have been impossible for him to look forward to going away. On return, he would normally have lots of outbursts, as already mentioned, and this would take a couple of weeks, at least, to settle. When he comes back from this vacation, the most we are expecting is that he will be a bit snappy and irritable, which is a huge step forward from damaging things in the house, hitting Mum and crying for hours.

REDUCING THE ANXIETY AROUND VACATIONS

What if your child is so anxious about going on vacation that you end up not going at all? This 'worst case' scenario is one that we would all prefer to avoid, and can avoid by implementing various strategies, such as 'practising' vacations, introducing them gradually, and encouraging your child to do some research.

Case study – Adam

'Holidays are a problem,' says Mum of Adam, who is aged 11. 'We only go for a few days as Adam gets really stressed, but he has an older brother who is 13 and he needs some quality of life too. Last year we booked on line and showed Adam where we were going, and he seemed excited to some degree. Yet as it got nearer the time of going, he started crying and he got really anxious and kept asking me, "What if I get ill?" I said we would take medicine, etc. and he would be fine. This year we are going for a week for the first time in years and I'm not too sure how he will be nearer the time...'

INTRODUCE VACATIONS GRADUALLY

Instead of taking your child with autism on vacation 'all in one go', try introducing the time away from home gradually. You can start with an afternoon or day out, and build it from there – maybe staying away from home overnight to begin with, and gradually increasing this to a weekend away. This is not as simple as it sounds, but using the transition techniques described in this book should help to reduce some of the confusion and apprehension your child experiences.

Practice

You can practise things such as packing and taking a bus, taxi or car drive to the train station or airport. This may seem a bit excessive, but a gradual introduction to such a different routine and to such busy places really can be helpful for your child, and will make life easier for you and all of the family in the long run.

If children are able to practise vacations in this way, it is important that they get lots of praise to help build their self-esteem and confidence in this area. If you do take them to a place where they may experience sensory overload, such as a train station, try to give them some resting time when they return home. Don't add to the overload by asking lots of questions or talking to them too much; we have made this mistake so many times, and still do! It is probable that children with autism will experience sensory overload when visiting such noisy and chaotic environments, and they will need some quiet time on their return (see Chapter 4, 'Sensory Overload').

Do some research

Encourage your child to research the place to which you are going. You could do a small project on it in advance of the day trip or weekend away or vacation:

making notes, drawing pictures or maps and fact finding. You and your child can use the library or the internet for this.

You could also do some research on the history of vacations, finding out when, why and how they began. Often children with autism like facts, and gathering information can help a child to focus on something of interest rather than something that may trigger anxiety. We often find that when our son is absorbed in something of interest, he is less likely to feel anxious about what is going on around him and less likely to obsess about future events.

Meeting the needs of your other children

If you have other children and their quality of life is being affected by the anxiety of your child with autism, you will obviously be torn when trying to meet the needs of each of your children. This is a difficult one, and there are no easy answers. If you are a two-parent family and have the money to do so, you could try taking the children away separately, taking the child with autism on a shorter trip and the other children on the sort of vacation they want to go on. This doesn't sound very nice, and you don't want anyone to feel left out or left behind. We are not suggesting segregation for children with autism, just some breathing space for them to 'practise' going on vacation until they feel confident enough to go away for longer periods of time. Maybe it's possible for your other children to go away with grandparents or other family members while you are building up to vacations with your child who has autism. Of course this situation wouldn't be ideal, but sometimes it helps to do things in stages with a child who has autism, and vacations are no exception.

Acknowledge your child's anxiety

Encourage anxious children to talk to you about the things that worry them regarding vacations, and always take their anxieties seriously, even if they sound silly or trivial to you. Using the transition techniques of making notes and drawing can help children to communicate their worries to you. It may be that your child is unable to tell you what is wrong. Even incredibly articulate children with autism are often unable to explain how they feel. If children do attempt to let you know how they are feeling, show them how pleased you are that they have been able to do this, or have at least tried. It is often so hard for our children even to recognize how they are feeling, let alone communicate those feelings to someone else. Any effort by your child to express his or her feelings should always be recognized and welcomed by you.

TO SUM UP

- Talk in advance with your child about the vacation. Make notes and draw pictures showing how things are now, and the changes that will take place on vacation.

- Create a vacation record book: make notes and draw pictures about what your child is looking forward to about the vacation, and what he or she will miss about home.

- Take the vacation record book away with you and use it to keep a diary with your child about the vacation. Fill this in regularly.

- Before you return home, make notes and drawings with your child about the vacation coming to an end, and what he or she might miss about being on vacation.

- Make notes and draw about how things will be different again when you return home; for example, 'I will go to school' or, 'I won't get to eat ice-cream every day!'

- When you have been home for a few days, talk, write and draw about how things have been since you returned from vacation, remembering to pick up on and praise any effort made by your child to be calm or to cope with anxiety during this time of transition. Refer to the vacation diary and talk about how things were on vacation and how they have changed now you are home.

Bob's comments

In the past, coming back from vacation was very, very stressful for all of us. There were obviously some things that were good about day-to-day life, for example, no sun cream! And seeing the dogs was great. But I couldn't stay up late, or have as much ice-cream and chocolate, and there was definitely no beach or sea!

I was not able to express my emotions, except in the most basic way, through my behaviour. I was often rude and aggressive for up to two weeks after a vacation. This was simply because the change from daily life to vacation life and then back again was too great.

The transition techniques have obviously helped with this. Nowadays there are no real outbursts when we are back from vacation. Occasionally, I may be a little snappy or quiet because I am tired. There are no ways I can find to express why they are helpful. They just are.

The use of these techniques would obviously differ greatly based on the family, and where you are travelling to. You would need to consider the needs of a sibling that does not have autism in whatever techniques or plans you are implementing for your child who does have autism. For example, you may decide that the child with autism may react better if he or she was taken away on the family vacation for one week instead of two, but this obviously would not be fair on the non-autistic siblings, that they can only go away for one week instead of two because their brother or sister couldn't handle it. This would only cause resentment and you would still have to deal with the change.

Sometimes going on vacation is like going through the portal in the film *Being John Malkovich*, but instead of seeing the world through someone else's eyes, you are able to escape from all of the responsibilities of your everyday life; and if you happen to go abroad you get the added bonus of sun and a nice warm sea to swim in. Like the characters in that film, when the experience ends, your everyday life may seem dull and grey by comparison. This makes it extremely hard to settle back into, and pretty much as soon as you get home you want to go straight back on vacation. You are on holiday, then all of a sudden, you get on a plane and in a matter of hours you are back home. The post is piled up on the doormat and the fruit you accidentally left in the bowl is starting to go mouldy, and it's most probably raining, and you are expected to get right back into your everyday life! This might not be easy for anyone, but if you have autism it can be even more difficult. It probably took you two or three days to adjust to being on vacation, and then suddenly, just when you are starting to get into it and relax, it all changes once more. This might paint a pretty miserable picture of going on vacation with a person who has autism, but that is actually far from the case. It might take you a bit more time to plan and prepare for it and you may still have a lot of work to do when you get back, but it will be worth it.

Sometimes when we are on vacation, arguments are likely to occur for all sorts of reasons. Some people like to plan lots of things to do on vacation, but at the same time they like to enjoy the freedom to change these plans at short notice. Now as I already said, this is not the best thing to do for a person with autism. So sometimes, when we have a plan for the day and midway through, my dad completely changes it, this annoys me; but because I am relaxed and on vacation, I don't react as I normally might, but I still show my anger at the change in plan. This has in the past created an unpleasant atmosphere. My dad has realized that changing plans at short notice is not a good idea, so now we either don't make plans for the day, or we make them and stick to them. This is good, because at times in the past, the tense atmosphere has made it feel as if we were Ray Winston and Ben Kingsley in one of the poolside scenes in the film *Sexy Beast*.

SOME MORE EXAMPLES OF TRANSITION TECHNIQUES USED FOR VACATIONS AND HOLIDAYS

Fuerteventura 2005

It is my tenth birthday on Friday 4th February. I will be on holiday. Dad and Mum are taking me on holiday because they think that being ten is a special birthday.

I have to get up at 3 am on Tuesday to get to the airport.

- How do I feel about getting up so early?

> Fine; I am excited about this.

- Am I looking forward to flying?

> I suppose it will be good.
> I am looking forward to having my breakfast on the plane.

- What am I looking forward to most about Fuerteventura?

> Beaches, pool, food, staying up late. I am looking forward to spending my birthday on holiday although I was anxious at first about this because I have never had a birthday away from home before.

- Who and what will I miss while I'm away?

> I will miss Fred.
> I will miss being at home.

- I have never had a birthday away from home before. What do I think about having a birthday away from home?

> Strange, in a good way.

- Do I have any questions to ask Mum and Dad about the holiday?

> No.

I will be in Fuerteventura for one week.

Figure 6.10: Preparing for holiday in Fuerteventura, February 2005

Fuerteventura 2005 continued

We have been in Fuerteventura for five days now.

We will return home on 8th February.

Fuerteventura is one of the Canary Isles.

It is Spanish.

I also came here when I was a toddler.

- Did I enjoy having my birthday away from home?
    Yes. We went to the beach. At night we went for a meal and I had pizza.

- What am I looking forward to about going home?
    Seeing Fred! ☺

- What will I miss about being on holiday?
    Sun, sand, sea, eating out.

- Is there anything I am not looking forward to about going home?
    Home education, going to bed earlier. ☹

Figure 6.11: Preparing to return home after holiday in Fuerteventura

Home education. We will build this up slowly over the week.

Bedtime will gradually come back to 9.30 pm over a week.

Being with the pets again.

We will try to go swimming more often for the first couple of weeks.

Gradual return to everyday life

Chocolate approximately twice a week.

Probably lots of rain.

We will try to eat out once a month, but not every day like we did on holiday!

Figure 6.12: What life will be like when we get back home

Fuerteventura 2005 continued

13th February 2005

We have been home for five days now.

- Am I glad to be home?

     Yes, I am.

- What do I miss about Jandia?

     Beach, pool, sun, nice food.

- What was the best thing about coming home?

     Seeing the animals.

- I start my home education again on Monday. Have I got any worries about this?

     No.

- Did Fred miss me while I was away?

     Yes.

Fred missing Bob

Figure 6.13: *Back at home after holiday in Fuerteventura*

London. April 2005

Travelling to London

1. Dad will collect Bob and Mum from home in his car and take them to his flat.

2. At 9.30 am we will all go to Dane Road metro station. We will get a metro to Piccadilly train station.

3. We will get a train at 11 am to London. We will get to London at approximately 1.15 pm.
   It is possible that the train will be delayed so we may get to London later than planned.

4. We will get the underground tube train to a station near to the hotel we will be staying at.

5. We will go to the hotel. We may need to get a bus.

Figure 6.14: Trip to London, April 2005

7

PUBLIC HOLIDAYS AND FESTIVALS

Christmas is supposed to be a happy time but we are starting to dread it more and more each year…

(Father of a nine-year-old girl with autism)

Whichever festival or holiday you celebrate, you will find that there is a lot of change in your home, your life and the community. You may have more social visits with people, exchange cards and gifts, and have family coming to stay. Often the food we eat at festivals and holiday times is different, routines change significantly, and the house may be decorated with a Christmas tree or other religious equivalents. Children will be off school or college, and parents may be off work. In fact, almost every aspect of your child's life will change to some degree around these times. It is quite normal for anyone, including neurotypical people, to become stressed at times of religious or cultural celebrations, and most people will find it difficult to return to work, college or school when the celebration is over. Some level of anxiety or low mood is to be expected. However, for people with autism spectrum condition, the change from their normal routine and the period of transition they have to go through in a short period of time is probably much more significant for them, and they may become particularly stressed, confused or even frightened.

This increased anxiety, along with the probable sensory overload they will experience with so much going on, will increase the likelihood of their displaying challenging behaviour. It is true to say, though, that any of us experiencing the level of anxiety that people with autism can experience during times of change would probably display quite a bit of challenging behaviour of our own!

If you are preparing to celebrate a particular festival or tradition related to your religion or your culture, and you think this may have a negative impact on your child, then you will want to do all you can to help to alleviate some of the anxieties your child is experiencing so that he or she can join in the festivities as much (or as little) as feels comfortable, and have a more positive experience.

This was certainly the case in our situation, which is why we developed the transition techniques to help reduce some of the distress that these changes during festival and holiday times were causing for our son.

Case study – Bob

Bob's family celebrate Christmas, and this has always been a particularly difficult time of year for them. Bob loves the excitement of Christmas, especially the food and the presents. However, just because he loves it so much doesn't mean he feels okay about it. He finds the transition from everyday life to Christmas and New Year hard to cope with and especially hard is the change back from the festive mood to the everyday.

In the past he had quite aggressive outbursts when the changes around Christmas time were taking place. The change in his routine was overwhelming for him. This led to all sorts of problems for Bob and for his parents. He would become very distressed, shouting and crying, yet not able to explain why. Christmas should have been a fun and relaxing time, but more often it was stressful and daunting for everyone.

On Christmas morning, he would open his presents and not react to them at all. His face would be blank and he would make no comment. His parents knew he loved his presents because they know what kind of things he likes, but it was hard to watch him not knowing how to react and not being able to show his feelings. He was probably overwhelmed by the amount of presents he received; but because things are so different on Christmas day than on any other day of the year, a sensory overload was almost inevitable.

He was most likely to have an emotional outburst in the period between Christmas and New Year, and after New Year, when things go back to normal.

An emotional outburst would normally include hitting, kicking, biting Mum and lots of shouting and crying. His parents managed to reduce these outbursts significantly by developing and implementing a reward plan (see *Create a Reward Plan for Your Child with Asperger Syndrome*). However, times of change still proved very challenging for their son, and so they decided to develop the transition techniques as well.

Transition techniques to help Bob feel less anxious and overwhelmed during the festive season

Please note: we are using Christmas and New Year as examples only, but feel that our transition techniques could work just as well for Ramadan and Eid, Diwali or any other time of change due to a tradition or festival.

Children with autism often benefit from information being presented in a very visual way. Keeping this in mind, we now prepare for Christmas and New Year well in advance. All we need is a sheet of paper and some felt tip pens.

- We sit down together and talk about how things are now, and what we do in our everyday life.

- We write this down and our son draws pictures next to each point. For example, if we write, 'We go to dog training on Tuesday evening', he will draw a picture of the dogs next to the written point (see Figure 7.1).

- We then talk, write and draw about what will be different over the Christmas and New Year period. For example, if we say that there will be no dog training over Christmas, then Bob will draw a picture of the dogs and draw a cross through the picture (see Figure 7.2).

- We will talk, write and draw about the things we normally do that we won't be doing, or will be doing differently; and about the new things that we will be doing. An example of this is visiting: there will probably be more social contact over the Christmas period as we deliver presents and have people deliver presents to us. Bob would therefore draw a picture of lots of people next to the point we have written about increased social contact (see Figure 7.2).

- We also use a big calendar, which we fill in and talk about in advance of the Christmas period, so Bob can see at a glance what is happening, and when, during this time of change. We make the calendar from a big piece of card, and illustrate it with Christmassy pictures. We leave large spaces for each day and space underneath the dates for making notes (see Figure 7.3).

Christmas and New Year transition

Everyday life - how are things now?

 Home education.

 Two bars of chocolate a week.

  Dog training.

Fred   Poppy

 No presents.

 Occasional visitors.

 No Christmas tree or decorations.

  Bed at 9.30 pm.

 Eating our usual meals.

  Some TV, lots of radio.

 I will go shopping sometimes with Mum.

 Dad will come as normal.

 I go out sometimes, for example, the theatre.

Figure 7.1: Everyday life – how are things now?

Christmas and New Year – what changes will there be?

 No home education.

 Eating more chocolate.

 No dog training.

 Getting lots of presents!

 More visitors to the house, possibly bringing presents!

 The house will look different, including a tree and decorations.

 Going to bed later. Getting up earlier sometimes.

 We will eat different foods, including turkey, crisps and sprouts!

 Lots of radio, lots of TV.

 Dad will do most of the shopping. I may go with him sometimes.

 Dad will be off work. He will come to the house more often. He will stay overnight sometimes (see calendar).

 I will go to the theatre and cinema more often.

Figure 7.2: Changes at Christmas and New Year

Monday	Tuesday	Wednesday	Thursday	Friday	Saturday	Sunday
					1st Bob and Dad to see Paul Merton at Lowry 2 pm.	2nd
3rd	4th	5th Dad and Bob to Sale History Group 7.30 pm. Mum going out with Linda.	6th	7th Haircut for Bob. Dad going out for a meal with work in the afternoon.	8th Carols at Walkden Gardens 2-4 pm.	9th Worthington Park Christmas Fair 11-3 pm.
10th	11th Dogs' Christmas party at dog club! 7.30 pm. Dad will stay overnight.	12th	13th	14th Dad starts Christmas holidays from work.	15th	16th
17th Dunham Massey with the home education group. Bob and Dad to cinema - Golden compass.	18th Dad going to football. Dad will stay overnight.	19th Last day of doing home education. Bob and Dad Xmas shopping. Dad will stay over.	20th Cinema - Nightmore before Christmas in 3D - Bob, Mum and Dad. Bob to visit Joseph at 5.30 pm.	21st Winter Solstice activities at Sale Water Park. Mum going out in the evening.	22nd Bob and Dad to see 'Hood in the Wood' at Royal Exchange 11 am, then spend afternoon in town centre.	23rd Bob and Dad to do the baking for Christmas. Bob, Mum and Dad to visit Grandma and Grandad in the evening.
24th Christmas Eve. Dad will stay overnight.	25th Christmas Day. Dad will stay overnight.	26th Boxing Day.	27th Dad goes back to work.	28th Mum to go out with Rebecca late afternoon.	29th. Dad's birthday.	30th Begin Transition techniques for transition from Christmas and New Year back to everyday life.
31st New Years Eve. Bob will stay up very late!!	 Dates to remember for January: 03.01.08 - Start home education slowly. 05.01.08 - Tom's Midnight Garden 2.30 pm - Mum, Dad and Bob. 26.01.08 - Poppy's 2nd birthday. 04.01.08 - Take Christmas decorations down. 06.01.08 - Bob's barium meal test.  					

Figure 7.3: Christmas calendar

These transition techniques have helped us enormously when it comes to helping our son to deal with the massive change in his routine around this time of year: diet, social life – everything! There are so many aspects of Bob's life that are disrupted by Christmas and New Year, it's no wonder he used to have such severe outbursts.

OTHER WAYS WE HELP BOB DEAL WITH FESTIVALS AND HOLIDAYS

Engage in fun activities

It can also help to do some fun activities with your child related to the festival that you and your family are celebrating. For example, in the weeks leading up to Christmas we would make all of the Christmas cards ourselves, just using scrap paper, glitter, paint, felt tips, crayons or cut-outs from old Christmas cards. This was an enjoyable way of introducing our son gradually to the idea that Christmas was approaching, and a way of helping him to relax and enjoy some of the preparation for it. His dad would make a Christmas cake, mince pies and some other treats that we know our son really likes and he would help to bake these things – and help to eat them! He would be proud of his contribution to the Christmas food and it gave him something to focus on and to become involved in. The intention was that this would go some way towards distracting him from thinking too much about all of the anxiety-provoking aspects of the changes that take place over the festive period. Of course, the change in food eaten over times of celebration could also cause problems for your child. He or she may not want to join in with the preparation of this food, or want to eat it, and of course you will have to respect this – every child is different.

Do projects about the festivity

We also do projects with our son around times of festivals and celebrations, including Christmas, Easter, Bonfire Night and Halloween. This is obviously educational and valuable from that point of view, but for us it has much more than an educational value. Again, it helps to focus our son's mind on something factual, interesting and enjoyable. He can find out lots of information about each subject, and this helps to keep him occupied and calmer than he would otherwise be if just left to his own devices to worry. We will usually help him to research the topic and he draws pictures, writes information, answers questions and anything else we can think of at the time to keep him interested and motivated. We usually then put a display on the wall of all the pictures, writing and facts he has put together related to whichever celebration we are focusing on.

As long as your child is willing, all this extra work is well worth doing. We have had a lot of success with our son during times of celebrations and festivals, and he has gradually become more confident in accepting and dealing with the changes that take place during these times. He does still experience some level of anxiety, but it is much less than it was. He is much more able to cope with the changes that take place and the transition that has to be gone through when faced with these occasions. He is also much more competent and confident at dealing with the feelings evoked when the celebration time is over, and everything goes back to normal.

TO SUM UP

Involve your child in writing the points and drawing the pictures, as this may help him or her to absorb and understand the information better. If your child doesn't want to do this, you can do it with your child watching. Try to involve your son or daughter as much as possible when you are doing the transition techniques.

If you or your child feel that he or she is too old for pictures, or just isn't happy about them, you can simply write the points. Alternatively, if the words are too confusing, you may just want to talk and use pictures with no writing. You can also use photographs or computer generated images. Do what suits your child.

If it is not too overwhelming for your child, it can be helpful to involve everyone who lives in your house so each person can play a part, as far as possible, in helping your child to get through the transition time as smoothly and calmly as possible.

In the weeks leading up to the festival or holiday:

- Talk and write about what your child already does every day (e.g., school, dance class, football practice).

- Draw pictures next to the written points.

- Talk and write about what will stay the same and what changes will take place over the coming festival or holiday period.

- Draw pictures next to these points. Include pictures of what your child normally does, and what will be new. Draw an X through the points or pictures that will not be happening over the holiday period (e.g., school).

Go over these points as many times as you need to leading up to and during the festival time, to help reduce your child's anxiety.

The transition from Christmas and New Year back to everyday life – what will change?

 Start doing home education again and build it up slowly.

 Two bars of chocolate a week.

 Fred   Poppy
Dog training will start again.

 No presents.

 We will have occasional visitors again.

 The Christmas tree and decorations will come down.

  Bedtime and getting up time will gradually go back to normal.

 We will eat our usual meals.

 Some TV, lots of radio.

 Sometimes I will go shopping with Mum.

 Dad will go back to work and will be with us as normal.

 I will go out sometimes to the theatre and cinema.

Figure 7.4: Changes from Christmas and New Year back to everyday life

During the festival time, start to talk about the transition back to everyday life (see Figure 7.4):

- Talk, write and draw about what is happening during the festival time. What is your child doing? (e.g., staying up later, eating more chocolate, going to a pantomime).

- Talk, write and draw about what will be different for your child when these activities are no longer happening.

- Talk, write and draw about how your child will be affected by change when the holiday time is over.

Remember, the change back to day-to-day life is just as important for your child. The more time and effort put into the transition techniques, the better the results you will see in your child.

Bob's comments

Christmas in itself has never been stressful, but the days leading up to it and following it have been. Although, obviously, the days after Christmas can be stressful for anybody – the thought that it won't happen again for another year – it is more so for me.

The transition techniques that we use are helpful, otherwise we wouldn't continue using them. Things used to be very difficult around Christmas time, before we started using the transition techniques, then within the space of a couple of Christmases, the changes were going by without us even noticing.

I'm not sure if this is the same for any other children with autism, but when I get presents I find it hard to give an emotional reaction to them (as described in Chapter 3, 'Emotions'), even when it's a really good present, for example, the *Matrix* DVD box set last Christmas. I had never seen the *Matrix* films before, so I didn't know if they were any good or not. Therefore, I felt a bit happy at getting some new films to watch, but couldn't properly express enjoyment about getting them until I had watched them. Does this make any sense?

Another example of a different situation is when I got the *Supernatural* box set (yes! more DVDs!) for my 13th birthday. A couple of years ago, when this had been on TV – it was the first series – I had been asking if I could stay up late and watch it, but had been told 'no'. This was partly because it was on too late, and also because my parents weren't quite sure if I was old enough to watch it. When I got this box set for my birthday, I was very pleased that I had it, and I knew it would be good because Mum had told me about the episodes after she had watched them herself on TV. But I still didn't show any particular reaction, except for perhaps a small smile, the same as I'd had for all of my presents. I can't quite explain why this is, but it doesn't really matter, because as long as you tell the person you like it and say thank you, then they'll know.

Obviously, I'm only talking about Christmas here because I can't talk about any festivals I don't celebrate, otherwise it would be patronizing and inaccurate information. Quite often, the hardest part is the beginning of January. All of the left-over food has been eaten and, although you still have your presents to continue playing with, it is still hard, having to get back to home education or school. It helps that I have a birthday in February, but January is still, more often than not, a dull month. One of the transition techniques that we've thought of is cutting back on the money we spend at Christmas and spending some of it in January instead, while gradually easing back into the day-to-day routine. An example of this is booking tickets for a play or pantomime to go and see in the New Year.

Perhaps Christmas is different if you celebrate it from a religious point of view rather than just presents and food, like me!!

8

OTHER

EXAMPLES OF TIMES OF

CHANGE

We have problems with change. Just a small change at school, for instance, can cause real upset. Last year they were having a 'silly hat' day at school for Children in Need, and Adam could not get to grips with or even try to imagine what was going to happen. He refused to get on his school bus.

(Lesley, mother of Adam, aged 11)

In this chapter, we explore further examples of times when the transition techniques may be of use to you and your child. These are not just random suggestions, but actual times of change that we have found challenging with our son, and that other people and their children have struggled with.

We have used the transition techniques with most of these situations and found them to be very helpful. This is not an exhaustive list, and you will probably be able to think of many other times in your child's life when our transition techniques can be used.

BIRTHDAYS

Most children get excited about a forthcoming birthday, but this is not always the case with children who have autism. It may be that they are not able to recognize or express the feeling of excitement, and this can come across as anxiety. Birthdays are another time of year when your child's routine might change: the house may be decorated with balloons and so on, there may be different food to eat, more people may be coming to the house, or a trip out may have been planned. The whole mood and atmosphere can change around the time of a birthday as you try to make this a special time for your child. Of course, you are doing what you think is best for your child with autism, just as you would do for a neurotypical child. It is hard for non-autistic people to understand that, what to them may be a welcome and exciting time, a time when they get to be centre of attention and are happy to be so, a child with autism may feel exactly the opposite. Children with an autism spectrum condition may actually dread their birthday, or at least experience some negative feelings as their birthday approaches. Unfortunately, they may not recognize or understand these feelings, or be able to express them in what is deemed to be an acceptable way.

Birthdays are meant to be happy times. But for your child, the changes around these times are many, often happen very quickly, and usually without any preparation or gradual build-up. This can create a lot of anxious feelings, such that your child may experience an emotional or sensory overload, so it should come as no surprise to us if he or she has an emotional outburst or meltdown. Some parents we have spoken to have told us stories of their children crying, shouting, throwing things, hitting and generally displaying some very aggressive behaviour. Other parents say that their children seem to 'go into themselves', becoming very quiet and unreachable. Neither of these situations is pleasant for the child to experience, or for us to witness. The following case study shows just how overwhelming birthdays can be for children affected by autism, creating sensory overload and impacting on their behaviour.

．．．．．．．．．．．．．．．．．．．．．．．．．．．．．．．．

Case study – Bob

One particular birthday that stands out for his parents is Bob's fifth – long before his diagnosis of autism. They had invited his grandparents and a few friends to a birthday tea. They had decorated the house with balloons, and placed birthday cards around the room. They had moved the dining table into the lounge, so the whole room looked different. Bob's friends were overexcited and very noisy, and his parents, friends' parents and grandparents were all 'cross-talking'. The atmosphere was very different from what Bob was used to. Normally, at that time in the evening, he would be at home alone with his mum, probably just reading.

Bob was initially very quiet, but then his behaviour became extreme. At one point he was on the landing, kicking and biting Mum, then he just sobbed and sobbed. His parents had no idea what was wrong with him. It was very distressing for all concerned, and his dad had to ask everyone to leave. Bob was inconsolable for the rest of the night and his parents were devastated by the whole experience.

If his parents had known about the autism then, things could have been so different – for a start, they never would have invited so many people! They could have kept the day as close to normal as possible, which always makes life easier. If they had done some preparation work with Bob in advance of his birthday to help him become aware of the changes that would be taking place, then he probably would not have become so overwhelmed and confused by the whole thing. That day stands out in his parents' life as a truly terrible day, one from which they all took a long time to recover.

Obviously you know when your child's birthday is coming up and so it is an ideal time to plan ahead for the changes that you know are inevitable, and put into place a variety of strategies.

Transition techniques

If the transition techniques had been available sooner, then Bob's fifth birthday would have been a really good time to use them. We could have created drawings and made notes about what would normally happen on that day, and then we could have drawn and made notes about what would be different because it was his birthday. We could have written a script or explained things by using a sketch, and made a sign for Bob to show us when he was starting to feel 'not okay'. Sadly, we didn't have the transition techniques in those days – we didn't even know Bob had autism! And so Bob got an emotional and sensory overload and metaphorically 'exploded' and we were left feeling like rubbish parents – knowing we'd got it wrong but not understanding how!

(Dad of Bob, aged 16)

Using the techniques illustrated in the earlier chapters, you can write, talk and draw about how things normally are and what will be different on your child's birthday. It may be a good idea to talk to family members and friends and ask them to be fairly precise about when they will be calling with cards and presents for your child. This will help you to prepare your child for any extra social contact. Alternatively, you can take control of the situation and tell people if and when they can come, especially if you know your child is likely to experience an emotional or sensory overload. The use of the transition techniques will help you and your child to get a better, more positive experience on your child's birthday.

...sion simple

... of pressure on parents these days to provide big, lavish parties for ...'s birthdays. Parties seem to get bigger and more extravagant as parents try to out-do each other, and that leaves us wondering who exactly these parties are for. The children would probably be happy with something that was much simpler!

Any child could be overwhelmed by such a big party, and a child with an autism spectrum condition particularly so. Don't feel pressured by other parents to give a party for your child if you know it wouldn't be right. Spending a fortune on an indulgent and excessive party is unnecessary – it doesn't prove your love for your child, and indeed, could be harmful. Only go ahead with a party if you know your child will love it, not because you feel you 'should' be doing it.

Spread out the present giving

It is so tempting to indulge our children on their birthdays as we would with a neurotypical child, but often children with autism will just feel overwhelmed if they receive too many new things at one time. It may help to spread the present giving out over days or even weeks to give your child the chance to get used to each new item. This may sound a bit extreme, but for children who thrive on routine and sameness, it gives them a chance to enjoy something new without experiencing too much anxiety.

Have your own celebration

Of course, you want to enjoy your child's birthday and it is a very special time for you as parents. Just because your child doesn't want to do something different or special on his or her birthday, you can still celebrate as parents by going out for a meal or doing an activity that means something to you to mark the occasion. You can still 'raise a glass' to your child!

CLOCKS GOING FORWARD OR BACKWARD

It's one hour, yet it can have a massive effect on children with autism. Their sense of security may be linked to their routine, so they may be very sensitive to these time changes. They may also have disrupted sleep, and their mood and behaviour can be affected for quite some time after the change. Our son is highly sensitive to the change in time when the clocks go forward or backward.

If you know that the clocks going forwards or backwards at the beginning and end of summer is likely to have an effect on your child, then you can prepare your child in advance by implementing a variety of techniques.

Use visual information to explain the changes

If you have been using the transition techniques for other things in advance of the clock change, then your child may be learning to be more confident with change and therefore more flexible. It is difficult to explain the clock changes to a child but you can try drawing this or using an actual clock to explain. Remember that children with an autism spectrum condition are likely to learn better with visual information, and so drawing a picture or a series of sketches to explain the clock changes to your child will probably help you to impart this information to your child in a fairly uncomplicated way.

The effect of tiredness on your child's emotions

When the clocks go forward at the start of summer, it may be that you need to prepare not only your child but also yourself, to get up an hour earlier. It is likely that your child will be tired, and this may be reflected in his or her behaviour for a few days or more after the time change. As we have talked about already on several occasions in this book, if your child is confused or distressed by this change, but unable to recognize or deal with these feelings, it is very likely to have a negative effect on behaviour. You may need to take this into consideration when making plans for your family, and try to schedule in some rest or quiet time for your child. We all get irritable and grumpy when we are tired, but most of us are able to acknowledge this and we know that it will pass. Your child with autism may need some help from you with understanding how he or she is feeling, and why.

Introduce the change of bedtime gradually

When the clocks go back at the end of summer, your child's bedtime routine may be affected, and he or she may find it difficult to go to sleep. Again, you can anticipate this and prepare for it. You can help your child to develop a pre-bedtime routine, such as getting into pyjamas, having a warm drink and a story before bed. If you try doing this an hour earlier than usual it may work, or it may not! You can try bringing bedtime forward gradually by ten minutes or so each night in the week leading up to the clock change, to help your child's body clock get used to the change. Alternatively, you can try keeping your child up an hour longer, so the clock says the usual bedtime, but it is in fact an hour later, as you have put the clocks back; then you can gradually bring this down by ten minutes a night until you are back to the original bedtime. In the short term, your child may be feeling more tired and therefore more irritable. Tiredness may cause increased stress and anxiety, and you may be feeling exactly the same – not a good combination! It is not easy to deal with these clock changes and it does require a great deal of effort from you – thought, planning, hard work and consistency; but as with everything else we do with our children, the more work we put in the better the result – usually!

THE CHANGING OF THE SEASONS

> A huge change for us is with the change of seasons, that is, dark and light, with or without a blackout blind. Light boxes are helpful but we still struggle…
>
> (Mother of Oliver, aged five)

Although the seasons appear to change gradually, there is a stark difference between them, and a multitude of changes. It isn't surprising that so many families who have a son or daughter with autism struggle during these times of seasonal change. Our children have to cope with a change of temperature, weather, the type of clothes they are expected to wear, the type of foods they are expected to eat and often, most problematic of all, the difference in the amount of light in the early mornings and evenings. One of the main problems with these changes, therefore, is sleep; children with autism often have issues around sleep anyway, and the changes of the seasons simply add to this problem.

Information reduces anxiety

The more knowledge and understanding your child has about the seasons, how they change and why, the less anxious he or she will be when experiencing each new season. This has certainly been true for our son. Knowledge allows us to make an informed choice; it empowers us. This is often the case for our children too. Even if some of our children understand things on a more basic level than others, we should still give them as much information as they are able to absorb.

It can be helpful and fun to do a project on the changes of season, or to make collages that depict the changes; for example, in autumn you can use fallen leaves. You and your child can also make up poems or stories related to the change of season. It is probable that your child's school will do similar things already, but if you are working one-to-one with your child, you can take it at your child's pace, so that he or she is more involved and will better absorb the information.

Transition techniques

Using the same transition techniques that we describe in Chapters 5 and 6, you can draw and write with your child about the season you are in, as it is coming to an end, and then draw and write about the forthcoming season: What will be the same? What will be different? How will all of this affect your child and your family as a whole? Try to keep it simple and to the point. You can do this over a period of days, or even weeks, and keep coming back to it. This should help to lessen any anxiety building up in your child.

We also use the transition techniques described in the previous section about the clocks going forwards or back. We make sure our son has a bedtime routine that will prepare his body for bed and sleep, and we stick to this as much as possible. If you know that your child, and therefore you, are going to lose sleep around the time that the seasons change, then you need to take this into account, as it could affect your child's behaviour and your response to that behaviour. You may not be as patient if you are tired. Try to rest when you can (easier said than done!). Accept help if it is offered, so that you can have a break and then come back more refreshed and better able to support your son or daughter. And try not to overschedule yourself or your child at this time in order to keep the risk of sensory overload to a minimum, and to give yourself the best chance of getting through this transition as smoothly as possible.

CHANGES OF BEDTIME

There are many reasons why your child's bedtime might change. It might be a permanent change: for example, because the child is growing up. It may be a temporary change: for example, the family needs to be up early to go on holiday, so the child needs to go to bed early. It could be that you are going for an evening out and you get home too late for your child to go to bed at the usual time. Whatever the reason, any change in the bedtime routine is possibly going to create some level of anxiety for your child.

Establish a bedtime routine

As mentioned previously, it is really important to have an established bedtime routine. Do you already have a routine that works for you? You need to prepare your child psychologically for bed so that he or she has slowed down, and is feeling relaxed and sleepy. Once you have a bedtime routine that works, this will help significantly when things have to change for some reason, whether that change is for one night or more permanently. As long as your child is skilled at preparing for bed, then no matter what change has occurred, he or she will still be able to fall asleep if you follow the bedtime routine as soon as possible after the change.

- Of paramount importance: is it possible that anything in your child's diet could be contributing to his or her sleep problems? It could be something containing particular E numbers (food additives), a sugar overload, or even a response to something seemingly healthy, such as bread, if your child has an intolerance of wheat or gluten. Any of these might be worth checking.

- Of equal importance: is your child comfortable? Is he or she warm enough; too warm; too cold? This may seem like an obvious thing to consider, but often people with autism can experience temperatures differently from neurotypical people (our son certainly does), so what may be a comfortable level of heat for you may be too much or too little for your child. Also, is your child irritated by the material of his or her nightwear or bedding? Material on skin can be very irritating to some people who have autism: they can be hypo- or hyper-sensitive to touch (see Chapter 4, 'Sensory Overload'), and this could be more than enough to affect sleep.

- Ensure that your child is not engaged in watching television, playing computer games or any other visually stimulating activity within one hour of bedtime; these activities will make it harder for your child's brain to switch off.

- Try to keep any play before bedtime calm and quiet leading up to the time your child will be going to sleep.

- Follow the same procedure at the same time each night. For example, if your child's bedtime is 8 pm, give your child a warm bath at 7 pm, followed by a warm, milky drink (but no caffeine). After teeth-cleaning, read to your child or let your child read to him- or herself. It can be quite cosy to do this in bed. Whatever the routine that suits your child, ensure that it is calm, relaxing and non-stimulating.

- It may help the bedtime routine if you have a sketch or series of pictures to show to your child so he or she knows what is coming next. For example, you might have pictures of a bath, teeth-brushing, putting on pyjamas, reading in bed, having a goodnight kiss, putting lights out, and so on. Present the individual pictures or sketches in order, and accompany them with verbal instructions, such as, 'First you will have a bath, and then you will brush your teeth'. Take this at your child's pace, and try not to overload him or her with too much information or too many instructions in one go. It's important to get the balance right between giving your child notice of what's coming next without making him or her feel pressured. You will only achieve this with practice as it will be different for each child.

- Lavender oil on a tissue near the bed can help to create a peaceful atmosphere (if your child is happy with the smell).

- Keep the lights as low as possible while you are carrying out the bedtime routine.

- If you have to change the bedtime routine for some reason (e.g. because your child is ill or you go on holiday), try to get back to it as soon as possible. You may need to do this gradually, but try not to let things slip.

- Some children with autism have great difficulty in sleeping. It can be hard to get them to bed and to leave them there alone. We created a 'bedtime plan' for our son for these reasons. The details of this bedtime plan can be found in our first book, *Create a Reward Plan for Your Child with Asperger Syndrome*. The bedtime plan took weeks to create and months to carry out and be successful. It was an incredible amount of work and we had to be very consistent. We all tried so hard to make it work, and gradually it did. It was a very structured plan and not intended to work overnight, but to increase our son's confidence in being upstairs and in bed by himself, over time. He went from sleeping with Mum to sleeping in his own bed with Mum in his room, and eventually to falling asleep alone, with Mum downstairs. He was ten at the time. He is 16 now, and these days he could fall asleep anywhere and sleep through anything!

- We used a blackout blind in our son's room. This helped to keep the evening light out in summer and the morning light out all year round. We also kept his bedroom door open and the landing light on all night, which helped him to feel safe.

- If your child is willing, you could use a relaxation CD to play while he or she is falling asleep. We haven't tried this with our son, but Mum has a hypnotherapy one which really works for her!

- Our son has dyspraxia, and so has some level of sensory deprivation. He likes to wrap himself up in his quilt cover – a bit like being in a sleeping bag – and this helps him to sleep. If this wasn't working for him, then we would have bought him an actual sleeping bag to snuggle up in. Some companies make weighted quilts for people who have this need for deep pressure, and you should be able to find details of these on the internet, or ask your child's occupational or physiotherapist if they have one. We haven't had need of one up to now but have heard very good reports of them.

- If your child's routine is going to change, for whatever reason, then using the transition techniques of drawing and making notes about how things are now, and how things will be after the change, can be very helpful. These techniques should work for the change in bedtime routine just as well as they work for some of the other smaller, more regular changes that we talk about in this book.

- Encourage your child to be as physically active as possible – an active child will be a tired child (one would hope), and physical exercise does release 'feel good' hormones that should help your child to feel more relaxed in general.

- Use signs, scripts and sketches wherever they may be helpful (see Chapter 9). You can create scripts to explain issues around bedtime to your child; or use sketches to help with his or her understanding of what is going on; or signs to help an awareness of what will happen next. In this way, you may find that the information is accepted and understood at a deeper level – especially if you are using visual aids.

- If you are experiencing problems around bedtime and sleep with your child, it may be useful to make notes about the problems as they occur. This may enable you to see if a pattern is forming and so give you a clearer idea of what is causing the difficulties for your child.

PARENTS OR FAMILY MEMBERS BEING OFF WORK WHEN THEY WOULDN'T NORMALLY BE

Planned

If the person's time off work is expected, this is easier because you have time to prepare your child. Using transition techniques, you can explain why things are going to be different for a while. It may sound ridiculous to prepare your child for Mum or Dad being off work when your child loves to spend time with Mum and Dad; however, it isn't about how your child feels about you, it's about helping him or her to deal with change.

There will be a transition to be gone through for your child to get used to Dad or Mum, or another family member or guardian, being off work; and another transition to be made when that person goes back to work. It may be hard for your child to recognize the fact that he or she may miss a parent, for example, when that parent has gone back to work. Your child may not be able to articulate this, and his or her unexpressed feelings may manifest as anger or distress. We could guarantee that whenever Dad went back to work after being at home with our son, our son would have a big emotional outburst.

The transition techniques really helped here because we were able to prepare him for the change of Dad being home when he wouldn't normally be, and then prepare him again for the change of Dad going back to work.

Unplanned

Dealing with unplanned things, such as illness, is always harder because you don't have the preparation time. However, you can use the same transition techniques in this situation as you would do for the planned time. Try to take some time out with your child and do a few sketches and notes about his or her normal routine, and how it will be different when the working parent is at home. For example, you may want to say that Dad will be here when the child gets in from school, or that Mum will be in bed when the child gets up in the morning. To enable your child to absorb the information more readily, encourage him or her to do the drawings if possible (the standard is not important as long as you and your child both know what they mean). Remember to do drawings and notes to explain the return to normal routine when the person is going back to work.

TRADESPEOPLE COMING TO WORK IN YOUR HOME

Having tradespeople in your house will be very disruptive for the whole family, especially if it's a big job such as having a new kitchen fitted or building work done. Even if it's just a small job, such as a plumber fixing your toilet, it can still be very anxiety-provoking for your child with autism.

If you have sufficient notice, you can use the transition techniques to prepare your child for the idea of having someone strange in your home. We did this when we were having a kitchen fitted in our old house, and electrical work done in our new house. The transition techniques helped our son to understand that things would be different for the period of time that the workperson would be in our home; that there would be some disruption and what that disruption would be. It also helped to reassure him that things would go back to normal once the plumber, electrician, kitchen fitter and so on, had finished their work, and left. He still doesn't like it when new tradespeople come to our home and usually stays in his room, but he seems better able to cope with the change of routine caused by having someone to work in the home. Also, we have some people who come back regularly, and he is now used to these people and hardly fazed at all when they come.

One problem is that our son doesn't always distinguish between friends and work people if they've been working in our house for a while. He'll say things such as, 'Aren't we sending the electrician a Christmas card?' This misunderstanding can be incorporated into the transition techniques; we can explain that we have different kinds of relationships with different people, and while it is probably okay to talk about personal things with a close friend, it probably isn't a good idea to tell the plumber about Mum's piles or Dad's wind (yes, he did!).

A FAMILY MEMBER GOING INTO HOSPITAL

This scenario can create major changes for your child. While the family member is away there will be hospital visiting, and recovery time once the family member comes home. This will be particularly significant if the family member lives in your home with your child. However, it can also have an impact if the family member doesn't live with you (e.g., a grandparent), but your child is expected to visit the person in hospital. This can also impact on your child if Mum or Dad, or other main carer, will be at the hospital a lot of the time and therefore away from home and the child.

Case study – Bob

Bob's uncle was in intensive care, in the burns unit, for six months. He wasn't expected to survive, and obviously Bob's mum needed to be at the hospital as much as possible with her brother. For the first few months, Bob didn't want to visit his uncle as he felt that there would be too many people and he felt anxious about going to the burns unit. He had to go from being with his mum all day to hardly seeing her at all, and being with his dad instead. As Bob was home educated, this had a massive impact on him as he was used to spending most of his time with his mum.

The transition techniques really helped here, as initially Bob couldn't understand why his mum needed to be away from him and with her brother. He was angry with his uncle for 'causing a fire' (his uncle actually did cause the fire, but not deliberately!) and therefore messing up his routine. It seemed as though Bob really was genuinely angry with his uncle. It is probable that his response manifested as anger because he was experiencing a myriad of emotions, some of which he had probably never felt before – such as shock. The whole family was in a state of shock, and it must have been so confusing for Bob to see his mum and his grandparents so distraught and so helpless. The emotional whirlwind going on inside Bob caused him to be very snappy, even aggressive, and to come across as completely uncaring and selfish, though Bob is neither of these things.

Use of the transition techniques and a script really helped him to feel less anxious about his mum being away, and also to feel less anger toward his uncle. They helped him to make sense of the situation and to see it (to some degree anyway) from his mum's point of view. It didn't help that Bob and his mum had moved house only a couple of months before the fire, and Bob was still getting used to that massive change. His dad was decorating the new house and so changes were going on all around him. All in all, we think Bob coped really well with the situation. Without the transition techniques, however, it is likely that Bob would have struggled with these changes far more than he did.

One of the main things a child may have to get used to when a family member goes into hospital is that his or her primary carer might change for a while. This is bound to have a big effect on the child, and the transition techniques we use would help to prepare a child for this.

The transition techniques could also be used to prepare children for going into hospital themselves, though this is such a major event that you may want to seek advice from the National Autistic Society, or a similar autism organization, to get the best advice.

VACATION FROM SCHOOL OR COLLEGE

It may be difficult for your child to go to school or college each day. Equally difficult is the transition from weekdays to weekends, or from the structure of term time to the less structured school holidays, and back again.

Your child's entire routine will be thrown into disarray and he or she will need some help from you in preparation for this period of transition. This is a really good time to use the transition techniques we developed for our son. If you take some time to write and draw about how things are now and how things will change over the vacation time, you will probably save your child from experiencing significant anxiety. Of course, your child is likely to experience some level of apprehension, but by using the transition techniques to explain what this time of change will mean for your child, you will be reducing some of the negative feelings he or she is facing.

All of the above situations will be experienced by most children at some point in their lives. We have learned that, often, preparation is the key to easing yourself and your child through the stress and confusion of change.

WHEN CHANGE OCCURS WITHOUT WARNING

If things change quickly and you don't have advance notice of change, our transition techniques are so simple that you can use them at short notice to great effect. An example of this from our lives is when our son's grandmother had a minor stroke and was rushed to hospital. Mum had to go to the hospital but Dad took some time out to do the transition techniques with Bob. Together, they drew some pictures of what had been planned for that day, and of what would actually be happening. Our son then crossed out the pictures of the things that wouldn't be happening now because of the change of plan. This really helped him to get some understanding that circumstances can change without warning, and that plans may have to change at short notice. By using these techniques, our son was able to learn that, yes, things may change suddenly, but with a little help he would be able to deal with these changes. The more practised you are at using the transition techniques when you have notice of change, the easier it will be for you to use them for any change that happens suddenly.

TO SUM UP

- Transition techniques – the simple formula of writing and drawing with your child about how things are now, and how things will be during and after a change takes place – can be used to help your child in most situations.

- Tailor the techniques to suit your child, depending on his or her age or ability. Drawings can be simple stick figures, or more detailed. You can be as creative as you like; you can use glue, glitter, decorations, photographs, cut-outs from magazines and so on.

- Keep transition techniques as compact and simple as possible to help your child to absorb, understand and retain the information.

- When change is predicted, you can prepare your child's transition period in advance.

- When change is sudden or unexpected, you can still use transition techniques, as they are so simple and only require pen, paper and a short amount of time to complete.

- The more you practise using the transition techniques for changes you can predict, the more familiar these techniques will be to your child, and the easier it will be for you to use them at short notice.

- Consider keeping the drawings, sketches and notes you have made, so that you can go over them again if necessary.

- There are numerous examples of small changes that your child will encounter at any point. We have used our transition techniques for all sorts of changes, big and small, and they have really helped us all.

Bob's comments

Even though the things listed here are only examples, they still go some way towards showing how change enters every person's life. For the most part, people don't even notice this change, or if they do, it doesn't have a particularly big effect on them; but if you are reading this you already know that this is not the case for people with Asperger Syndrome or autism. There will be many events that happen in your own lives that you won't find talked about in this book, but you can transfer the techniques found in here on to anything in your individual life, whether it's something that happens daily or yearly. But it is also important to take in to account your child's opinion. If, for example, they have tried the transition techniques and found them to be helpful for two or three Christmas's running, and then one year decide they do not wish to use them any more, it is important that you do not force them to do so, as these techniques are not about holding children's hands to get them through change throughout their life. They are really about getting them to deal with change in a calm and effective manner, and, in their adult life, perhaps even to embrace it. Even if choosing not to employ the transition techniques that year proves to be the wrong decision, and your child has an outburst, this will not put you back to square one, as you might think. It will in fact serve to reinforce all the good that has already been done with the transition techniques, by reminding you quite how good they actually are. If you use the transition techniques for long enough in a structured way, then eventually you may get to a point where you are able to deal with change without even thinking about it, or using any techniques at all. An example of this is when I had arranged for my friend Jake to come round at 6 pm one Friday night. When I opened the door to him, he was standing there with another friend whom I'd never met. At one point, when I was younger, I might have struggled to cope with this sudden change of plan, but now, after using the transition techniques for so many years, it didn't even bother me. And we all just went upstairs and watched the film *Cloverfield*. We then went out and met up with Jake's brothers and played football. This wasn't part of the original plan either, but I was fine through the whole thing. It didn't even occur to me that in the past I wouldn't have been, until my mum pointed it out. It's not that the transition techniques have got me to a point where I can cope with these smaller changes, it's that I don't actually need to 'cope' any more.

PART THREE

————————————————————————— ·····

ADDITIONAL TECHNIQUES AND STRATEGIES TO USE AT TIMES OF CHANGE AND WITH AUTISM IN GENERAL

9

SCRIPTS, SIGNS AND SKETCHES

Even the smallest change in our routine – for example, if I want to call at my sister's house when I pick her up from school, instead of going straight home – makes her stressed and anxious. I just don't know how to get it across to her, you know, that we'll be doing something different but that things will still be okay.

(Father of a nine-year-old girl with autism)

In our first book, *Create a Reward Plan for Your Child with Asperger Syndrome*, we included a chapter on additional techniques that we use to support our reward plan with our son. We also use these additional techniques – namely, scripts, signs and sketches – to support our transition techniques, and so feel it will be useful to include a chapter on them in this book.

SIGNS

It is often said that children with autism respond well to visual information. Signs offer an immediate and very visual form of interaction with your child. The sign can be of anything, depending on your child's particular needs at that moment. Signs offer a quick reminder to your child about something you have talked about or something you may have written a script about.

Case study – Bob

Bob used to get really anxious waiting for Dad to come from work. He hated not knowing exactly what time Dad would be coming, and of course we couldn't be precise. We made a 'Dad will be coming later' sign, which our son used to hold when he was starting to feel anxious. It helped to remind him that Dad would be coming soon, but we couldn't say exactly what time.

Signs are not a new idea when working with children who have autism. We have been using them for a long time as a family, since before our son's diagnosis of autism. We find them very helpful. We always draw our own signs, so that they are specific to our circumstances. Sometimes our son will design the sign and sometimes we will, or we may design the sign together. You can also use cut-out pictures or photographs to make your signs if you choose to. If your child likes the computer then you can download images from the internet to use as signs. Just use your imagination and take into account the sort of thing your child likes, and you will find something that suits you and your son or daughter.

Signs can be used in many situations to help your child to stay calm and to offer him or her support – a gentle reminder of what you have agreed together, or a more practical reminder of what is coming next. For example, when going on holiday you can have a sequence of signs to prepare your child for travelling: pictures of a taxi, an aeroplane, a hotel, and so on (see Chapter 6). At festival times, you could have a sign with people on for when visitors are coming, or a sign to show how the house will change with decorations.

And you will probably find that just holding the sign can be comforting for your child.

Figure 9.1: Letting go of an argument: the sign

SCRIPTS

We have been using simple scripts to explain things to our son since he was very small, long before we knew he had autism. It just seemed like such an obvious way to get information across in a clear but concise way.

When you want to explain something to your child, for example, that there will be more visitors coming to the house over the Christmas period, just think about what you want your child to understand from this:

- There will be more people coming to the house over Christmas to give and receive presents.

- The house may be noisier.

- More people will want to speak to the child.

- The child may not want to speak to people and may feel overwhelmed.

- If the child feels overwhelmed it is okay to go to his or her room for some quiet time.

Then just put these points into a short script.

More visitors over Christmas and New Year: the script

At Christmas, people may want to spend time with other people that they care about. They may want to give and receive cards and presents.

Often, people are off work or school and want to spend their spare time with family or friends.

This means that more people may be coming to our house over Christmas and New Year than at other times of the year.

When the house is busier than usual, it is possible that I may feel overwhelmed by the noise and the extra social contact.

Mum and Dad will try to make arrangements for visitors in advance so I can be prepared for them. However, on occasion, people may just 'turn up'.

I may not feel like speaking to people. I may want some peace and quiet when the house is busy.

If I start to feel uncomfortable or unhappy in any way, then it is okay for me to go to my room for some quiet time.

It may be hard for me to recognize how I am feeling, so Dad and Mum will tell me if they think I am starting to experience a 'sensory overload', and they will quietly suggest that I spend some time alone in my room.

(December 2007)

This is quite a long script. It would probably be better for most children, no matter what their age or ability, to have this script broken down into two or more scripts. It did work for our son, but may have been more helpful as two shorter scripts.

Of course, how you write the script will depend on the age and understanding of your child. However, even with an older or very intelligent child we find that it is still best to keep the script brief and to the point. You need to keep it simple, which is more likely to get the message across to your child.

Scripts can be used alone but we find they are often more effective when backed up by something visual such as a sign or a sketch (see following section).

Figure 9.2: More visitors over Christmas and New Year: the sign

When our son is going through the transition, for example, of vacation mode to everyday mode, we often use the 'staying calm' script and the 'let's calm down' sign to help him through this time of change. Of course, we also use the transition techniques discussed in Chapter 6. We often find that using more than one strategy and combining techniques works really well for our son.

SKETCHES

Sketches are also something we have been using to give information to our son since he was very young, and long before his diagnosis of autism. We have always drawn things as a way of explaining them to him. This has proved really useful as his autism emerged and it became apparent that visual information is very effective for him.

Below is an example of a sketch that you may wish to use with your child if there are likely to be more people visiting your home, for example during a festival or public holiday.

People who are usually in the house

Over Christmas and New Year more people may come, possibly bringing presents.

Bob feeling OK!

Too much noise for Bob!

Bob can go to his room for some quiet time.

Figure 9.3: More visitors over Christmas and New Year: the sketch

You don't have to be a good artist to use sketches with your child. Mostly, it simply involves people and speech bubbles. You can draw a picture or a series of pictures then show them to your child. However, you are more likely to get and maintain your child's attention if you do the drawings with your child (you may want to practise beforehand). The more involved the child is, the more likely the information is to be absorbed. If you are really not happy about attempting even the most basic of drawings, then it may be possible for you to do a sketch style illustration using cut-out pictures or photographs, though this may take you longer and be a bit more complicated. It may also be possible to obtain pictures from the internet.

Sketches can be very simple and yet still convey lots of information to your child. It can even be that the simpler the sketch, the more your child will get the message, so don't bother including too much detail.

ENCOURAGING YOUR CHILD TO RESPOND TO SCRIPTS, SIGNS AND SKETCHES

If you are using any of these techniques, remember that your child may not respond to them straight away, so reward any effort at all, however small – lots of praise is always a good reward. Acknowledge any positive attempt your child makes when trying to deal with the stress and turmoil that he or she experiences during times of change and transition. Your child may not be successful, but is more likely to keep trying if his or her efforts are not going unnoticed.

Case study – Bob

If he responds positively to a script, sign or sketch – for example, if he calms down quickly or lets go of an argument – then Mum or Dad will give him points for his reward plan. He will be rewarded if he makes any attempt to use these techniques, as he doesn't always respond to them straight away. The 'let's calm down' sign took a lot of time and effort to work. For example, Bob was rewarded initially just for looking at this sign, and if he took just a little less time to calm down than usual. Eventually he started to respond to this sign almost straight away, but only if it was shown quickly enough to him, before his anger got 'too big'.

COMBINING TECHNIQUES

We often combine techniques to give maximum support to our son. Below are two examples of instances where we have used a combination of signs and scripts to help him in his interactions with Mum.

Case study – Bob

Bob uses a 'calming down' sign, a 'letting go of an argument' sign and a 'shush' sign amongst others. Here is an example of how one of these signs is used: Bob will argue about anything continuously, for hours sometimes! He is unable to settle until his mum has admitted that he is right and she is wrong. Of course she can't always do this – that would be giving into him and leaving him thinking that there is only ever one side to an argument – his! If he is becoming too distressed then sometimes she does have to 'give-in' and the issue has to be sorted out later, when they are both calm.

We wrote a script and made a sign to show to him when he is refusing to let go of an argument. This was very important because he can get increasingly frustrated with his mum and this eventually leads to a big emotional outburst. After talking about the importance of sometimes 'agreeing to disagree' (a concept which Bob still has huge problems understanding), we wrote the script and made a sign for Mum to show to him whenever this situation arises.

This script and sign began to work straight away, as long as we showed Bob the sign early enough. If we left it too long and his anger was already underway, then it was a lot harder to get him to let the argument go. It was very helpful to us to use this script and the sign as they enabled us to sort out arguments before they got out of control, and before Bob had an outburst. They made us each take responsibility for our part in the disagreement and in trying to sort it out.

Letting go of an argument: the script

Sometimes Mum and I disagree.

I often get upset if Mum doesn't agree with me.

Mum says she can't say she agrees with me just to keep me calm, because then she wouldn't be telling the truth. Also, she would be giving into unreasonable demands. I find it hard to accept that Mum won't always see my point of view or say that I am right.

Because of this, I keep arguments going for a long time. I can't let the argument go unless Mum agrees with me.

This is so distressing for me that I get pains in my throat and chest.

Mum and Dad want to help me avoid getting to this point.

When Mum thinks that I need to let an argument go, she will show me my 'letting go of an argument' sign. We can talk about the disagreement later, when we are calm and relaxed.

If I respond to the sign by letting the argument go, Mum and I will be much happier. I will be pleased with myself if I respond appropriately to the sign and I will get points for my reward plan.

(April 2008)

Note: your child may still struggle with the idea that an argument doesn't have to be settled in that moment, but things will probably be easier for you if you use the above sign. If you talk about the issue later on, when everyone is calm, then at least you will all feel that you have been 'heard' and 'understood', if not 'agreed with'!

Listening to Mum: the script

Sometimes Mum needs me to listen to her. It may be that she has an important thing to tell me; for example, when we are doing my home education she may need to give me an explanation of what she wants me to do.

It is important that I listen to Mum so we can communicate properly and understand what we need from each other.
Sometimes I feel Mum talks too much and I don't want to listen.
Sometimes my mind feels overloaded and I just want Mum to stop talking or to use fewer words.

Mum will try to talk less and be more concise with her explanations. I will let Mum talk and not interrupt or say 'I know what to do', before Mum has had a chance to explain.

Mum can show me the 'I need you to listen to me' sign and if I can't listen just then I can explain calmly or show Mum the 'shush' sign.

Mum and I will fall out less if we do this, so we will be happier. Dad will be happier because he won't have to listen to Mum and me moaning about each other!

(February 2007)

Figure 9.4: Listening to Mum: the sign

SOME ADDITIONAL EXAMPLES OF SIGNS, SCRIPTS AND SKETCHES

Calming down: the script

Sometimes I feel a little bit annoyed.

This feeling can very quickly grow into anger.

When I get angry, I might say or do something that will hurt another person.

I might do or say something that will make me unhappy with myself when I am calm.

I can try to stop my anger from growing.

If Mum shows me my 'let's calm down' sign it might remind me to calm down before my anger gets too big.

If Mum starts to get angry I can show her the 'let's calm down' sign we made for her.

Together, we can try to deal with angry feelings without upsetting each other.

We will be very pleased with each other if we manage to do this.

(January 2005)

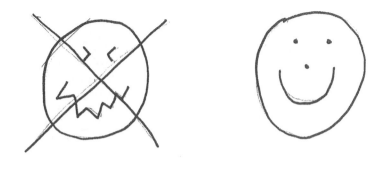

Figure 9.5: Let's calm down: Bob's sign

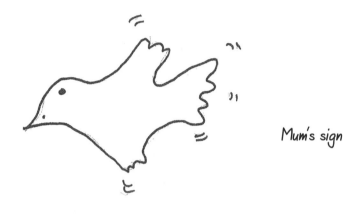

Figure 9.6: Let's calm down: Mum's sign

Shush: the script

It is rude to tell people to shut up.

The person who is being told to shut up can feel embarrassed and cross.

The person who is told to shut up then wants to talk even more, to defend him- or herself.

Sometimes I tell Mum to shut up.

I tell Mum to shut up because I feel that I need Mum to be quiet at that moment.

I may be feeling overwhelmed and am not able to explain this.

I can ask Mum nicely to be quiet by showing her my 'shush' sign.

If I don't have my 'shush' sign I can gently put my fingers to my lips.

Dad and Mum will be very pleased if I use my 'shush' sign and I will be pleased with myself.

(November 2004)

Figure 9.7: Shush: the sign

I need a break: the script

Sometimes when I am doing my home education, I start to feel unhappy. This could be a feeling of irritability, frustration, even anger. I don't always know what the uncomfortable feeling is.

In the past I have allowed the feeling to grow and have become angry with Mum.

I don't have to continue with home education if I feel like this. I can ask for a break or show Mum my 'I need a break' sign.

If I ask for a break or show Mum my 'I need a break' sign I will get a break immediately.

Home education can continue when I've had a break.

If I ask for a break or use my sign I will stay calm and Mum and I will be happy.

(2006)

Figure 9.8: I need a break: the sign

Using the bus: the script

Sometimes Mum and I need to use the bus.

Bus queues can be long and noisy.

Bus journeys can be noisy.

Lots of people need to use the bus.

People who use the bus have different needs and abilities.

At the moment I am finding this hard to understand and I don't agree with the social rules surrounding bus journeys.

If I become upset or angry this brings negative attention to Mum and me. It is important that I stay calm and quiet in the queue and on the bus.

Until I understand the situation better, I must trust Mum and be guided by her.

I must let Mum take the lead and do as Mum asks when at the bus stop and on the bus.

I must stay quiet and calm to keep Mum and me safe.

(2006)

Figure 9.9: Using the bus: the sign

Weekday to weekend mode: the script

On the weekdays (unless it's holiday time) most people get up early and go to bed early because they have school or college or work.

At weekends this changes for most people.

At weekends we do things differently.

We may get up later on Saturday or Sunday morning, and go to bed later on Friday or Saturday night.

We may stay at home for the day or we may go somewhere different; for example, to visit a friend or family member, or go to the park.

Most people will experience change in their routine as the week changes into the weekend. We will experience this change too.

(2008)

Monday

Tuesday

Wednesday

Thursday

Friday

Saturday

Sunday

Weekend comes to an end on Sunday night.

Figure 9.10: Weekday to weekend mode: the sign

Weekend to weekday mode: the script

At weekends we may have a quiet time or we may be busy, but weekends are always different from weekdays (unless it's vacation time).

On Sunday evening the weekend is almost over and it is time to prepare for the new week.

During the week most people begin their routine again of going to school, college or work.

People usually go to bed early on Sunday night so they can be up early on Monday morning.

(2008)

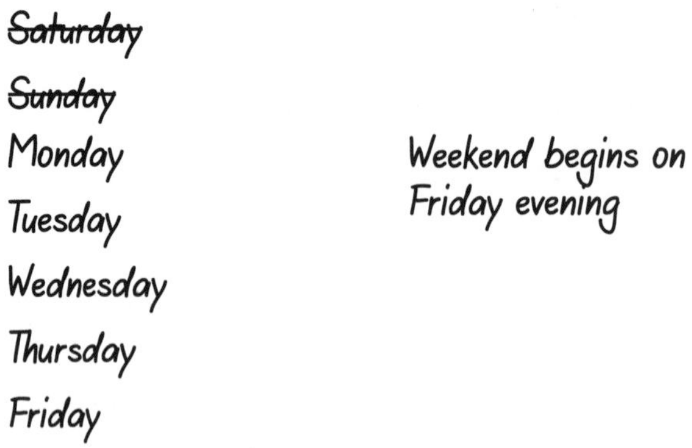

~~Saturday~~

~~Sunday~~

Monday

Tuesday   Weekend begins on
                           Friday evening
Wednesday

Thursday

Friday

Figure 9.11: Weekend to weekday mode: the sign

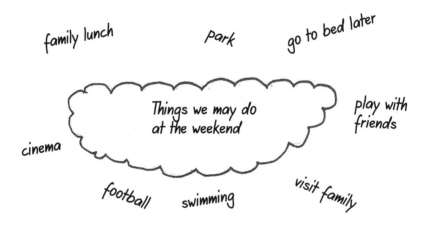

Figure 9.12: A weekend sign

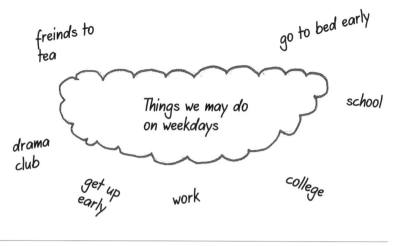

Figure 9.13: A weekday sign

SCRIPTS WE HAVE USED THAT DO NOT HAVE A SIGN TO GO WITH THEM

Mum going to the hospital: the script

Uncle Paul is very ill and Mum will have to go to the hospital to see him and to help Grandma and Grandad.

This means that Mum may be away from me for quite a few hours.

I don't like Mum going to the hospital, but I will try to understand that Mum needs to do this.

Mum will still look after me and I will still have all I need. If Mum can't look after me, then Dad will.

Mum will tell me approximately when she will be home from the hospital. If Mum is going to be late she will try her best to text or phone me.

I am trying hard to support Mum because I know she is very sad.

(August 2007)

Dealing with conflict with friends: the script

Sometimes I get cross with my friends. If they break the rules of a game or change the rules of a game, I feel upset with them.

I can sort this out by talking to my friends or asking a grown-up for help.

Sometimes I have to accept that my friends and I disagree. If I insist on being proved right my friends may fall out with me.

I must not shout or use any physical means (shoving, grabbing, pushing are examples).

I must deal with conflict calmly. My friends will respect me for this.

(March 2005)

Understanding that I can't control other people's facial expressions: the script

Sometimes, when I feel upset, agitated or overwhelmed, I get cross if Mum has a particular expression on her face. Sometimes I will tell Mum to change her facial expression or tell her to stop staring at me.

I am trying to learn that facial expressions are reflex reactions to certain feelings or moods.

I am trying to learn that sometimes people cannot control their own facial expressions, especially if that person is upset or angry.

The facial expression is a response to the person's feelings at that moment in time.

I could try to learn to understand Mum's facial expressions to help me work out how Mum is feeling. I might need some help with this.

I am trying to learn that people look at each other when they communicate, even in anger.

Sometimes I feel that Mum is glaring at me when she is angry.

Mum will try not to glare.

Dad and Mum will help me to learn more about facial expressions.

(2006)

On reflection, this script would probably have been better if we had split it into two: part one for the 'facial expressions', and part two for the 'glaring'. However, it was a helpful script.

Understanding that I can't control what other people say or do: the script

Sometimes I get a very strong feeling that I need Mum to do something or say something. I feel that I can't talk when someone is in a certain place or position. I can't explain why, but in that moment it feels crucial to me that Mum does as I ask.

Mum won't do as I ask if I shout at her, or if she thinks my request is unreasonable. Mum doesn't want me to 'get my own way' by shouting or using physical force.

If I do this, I am not treating Mum with respect. If I try to force people to do what I want outside of the home I could get into serious trouble.

Mum thinks I need to work through my anger by using my calming down techniques. I can talk to Mum and Dad about my feelings after the event, when I am calm.

Mum will not do as I ask if I try to force her, or if Mum thinks my request is unreasonable.

I have to accept this.

I have to calm myself down and then talk to Mum.

I will be very pleased with myself if I am able to deal with this feeling calmly in the future, but I may need some practice.

(2006)

Keeping calm in the shops: the script

I usually behave very nicely in the shops. This helps Mum to shop and keeps Mum and me safe.

Sometimes I see things on the floor or drop things on the floor in the shops. When I lie on the floor to look for things, I am blocking the aisle and I may trip people up. I may get hurt if someone stands on me or rolls their trolley into me.

I must not lie or crawl on the floor in the shops. If I drop something, I must ask Mum for help.

I may have to accept that I can't get something back if it has gone under the shelves.

I must behave nicely and calmly in the shops to keep Mum and me safe.

(September 2005)

How to attract attention: the script
Sometimes it may be difficult to attract someone's attention.

These are things I can try to help me to attract someone's attention:

I can try to say, 'EXCUSE ME'.

Usually, the person will look at me and they may say, 'Yes?' or 'Can I help you?' They may say, 'What do you want?'

It will be okay to say what I want to that person.

If the person doesn't reply, then I can say, 'EXCUSE ME' a bit louder.

It is important to attract someone's attention if I need their help. If I do not try to attract the person's attention I may not get what I want or what I need.

(2006)

Trying not to worry about the door being open: script one
Sometimes I feel anxious when the door is open.

This can be the kitchen or bathroom door, but it is most often the lounge door.

If I am in the lounge and the door is open, I find it hard to do my imaginings.*

I have to get up and close the door, or shout to Mum to close the door.

If Mum goes upstairs, I feel I have to shout up for Mum to check if my bedroom door is open.

Sometimes I shout up several times even though Mum has already checked for me.

It would be good to feel less anxious about the doors being open.

I could feel more relaxed if I didn't worry so much about the doors being open.

Dad and Mum, Alison and Christine* are going to help me feel more relaxed about the doors being open.

(March 2006)

---

*   Christine and Alison are Bob's psychologist and speech therapist.

Good things that could happen if I learn not to worry about the doors being open: script two

I wouldn't have to feel worried. Feeling worried is horrible (I suppose).

I wouldn't have to keep stopping what I was doing to get up and shut the door.

I could carry on with my imaginings** even if the door was open.

Mum wouldn't get cross with me about the doors, so Mum would be in a better mood, which would be nicer for me!

If I am not in such a rush for the door to be closed and I wait calmly until everyone is through before I close it, then there is less risk that Fred or Poppy*** will get caught in the door.

I will not have to keep getting up to let Fred in and out of the lounge.

(March 2006)

Good things that could happen if I leave things as they are: script three

There would be less work for me to do!

(March 2006)

The door being open was something we worked on with our son's psychologist and speech therapist. We have included them here to show how a script can be broken down into two or more scripts if it is in danger of becoming too long.

All of the above scripts, signs and sketches have been used by us to help our son to deal with various situations and areas of conflict as they have arisen. They are so much more effective than just talking to our child. It is difficult for people with autism to process too much verbal information in one go. The techniques of writing and drawing help to break down the information and offer it to your child in a much more manageable format. The strategies we have developed have enabled us to help our son, and while they are not miracles or cure-alls, and do take time, hard work and consistency, they are well worth implementing.

** Imaginings are something that our son does where he creates characters and stories in his head and he then puts these into the books he writes.
*** Fred and Poppy are Bob's dogs.

TO SUM UP

- Scripts, signs and sketches can be used in isolation, but are often more effective if they are combined, using two or even all three techniques.

- They can be used to help your child with every area of life, from self-care to social and communication skills, learning to be flexible and so on.

- Signs: are very visual and offer an immediate line of communication to your child. They are easy to carry around.

- Scripts: explain things simply, including how your child, or how other people, may be feeling in relation to whatever issue you are writing about.

- Sketches: can be used to explain things as you go along, writing and drawing as you talk, at your child's own pace.

- All of these techniques can be used as a backup to support the transition techniques that are discussed and illustrated earlier in the book. With practice, it won't be long before the scripts, signs and sketches, along with the transition techniques, become second nature to you when trying to help your child to deal with the things in life that he or she finds difficult.

Bob's comments

I mostly remember the 'shush' sign and the 'Dad will be coming later' sign, also the 'calm down so we don't upset the dogs' sign. They were all very helpful.

When I was home educated, I used to get very stressed and angry at times until we developed the 'I need a break' sign. I used to show this to Mum and then we would take a break until I felt calmer, so this helped to prevent a lot of arguments and calmed situations down.

We also used to use the 'let's calm down' signs. These were for when I did have an outburst and get angry at Mum. Mum would show them to me and they would help me calm down so the outburst wasn't as serious as it otherwise might have been. You need to use timing with these signs: there is no point in showing a 'let's calm down' sign to someone who is punching the wall and shouting their head off, but if you can see that they are heading to that stage, then the sign may be very useful to show them way before they reach that level.

Also, the 'let's calm down so we don't upset the dogs' sign was very useful for helping me to realize it wasn't just me and Mum who were being affected by our arguments, and how they might be scaring the dogs.

The 'letting go of an argument' sign was also extremely useful. We used it to stop us arguing in that moment, and agreed to talk about whatever it was we were arguing about later, when we were both calm.

10
GENERAL ADVICE

This book was written to offer help and advice to parents and carers who are trying to help their children cope with the smaller, more everyday changes that they are often faced with. However, life throws up many challenges for our children who have autism and therefore for our families as a whole. We thought it would be useful to look at some of these other issues and to offer some general advice from us to you on these subjects. We give case studies and examples from our own lives with our son, and we offer some helpful tips on how to deal with each issue. We don't have all of the answers, but if something has worked for us then it makes sense to share it with you, in the hope that it will help you too.

COMMUNICATION
Scripts, signs and sketches will help with communication between you and your child, especially when you are trying to get your child to understand something. But obviously, the manner in which you speak, and your body language are also important when you are interacting with your child.

Non-verbal communication
Most of our communication is non-verbal, that is, body language and facial expressions. This is unfortunate for people with autism, as their understanding of non-verbal communication is often very limited and has to be learned through experience and explanation.

Drawing facial expressions and using photographs and pictures from magazines can help. Also, soap operas on TV can be quite useful when teaching children about non-verbal communication. Talk to them about the way the characters use non-verbal communication as they interact with each other. Doing little role-plays with or for your child can also be a fun way of helping your child to learn more about non-verbal communication.

Non-verbal communication is such a massive subject that you may want to seek more detailed information or advice regarding this as we can only offer a brief outline here.

Keep verbal communication short and to the point

Through experience, we have learned that *how* we speak to our child plays a huge part in his understanding of what we want him to do or learn. It is important to recognize that this has nothing to do with intellect. Most people with Asperger Syndrome, for example, are of average or above average intelligence.

However, despite his fantastic brain, our son, like many people with autism, takes longer to absorb and process information than most neurotypical people. While we understand this, we still find ourselves talking too quickly and giving him one instruction after another without waiting for the first thing we said to be processed. Mum is the worst one for this. Bob always says that Mum talks too much and says 50 words when one will suffice!

Case study – Bob

Only this morning Bob said to Mum, 'Have you finished there?'

He wanted to get into the kitchen cupboards.

Mum said, 'Well, I was just going to put these apples in the bowl, but it doesn't matter. I can do it later. It won't make any difference if I don't do it now.'

Bob replied, 'So that's a yes, then?'

This is a typical example of Mum talking too much and giving Bob too much unnecessary information to process in one go. This incident sounds harmless enough, but multiply it by the number of conversations like this that take place every day, and it becomes easy to see why he has sensory overloads and is often snappy and abrupt!

The above example highlights that there is no need to 'waffle'. If you want to get information across to your child with autism, it is better to be precise and to the point. Speak clearly and slightly more slowly. Of course, this isn't always possible, but if you follow this rule as often as you can, especially if your child is anxious, or you are in a stressful situation, it can help to defuse things, or at least stop things from getting worse.

CHOOSE YOUR BATTLES

This saying is true with all children. Some battles are not worth winning, as the cost to the relationship with your child can be too high. If you persistently argue your point and have to be right all of the time, your child will feel as though his or her opinion is of little value. This is the case with neurotypical children, especially teenagers, but 'choose your battles' is very good advice indeed when dealing with your child who has autism.

If the issue isn't particularly important, then it's okay to 'give in' or 'agree to disagree'. Letting things go is often hard when we are in conflict with anyone, but it can be especially difficult with our children. As adults, we may believe that our children should listen to us, do as they're told, not answer back and not question our authority. But if you are the parent of a child with Asperger Syndrome, you will probably know by now that these expectations are not based on reality. It is usual for people with Asperger Syndrome to think logically (in a 'black and white' way); be very direct; and 'speak as they find'. This is one of the beautiful things about Asperger Syndrome – the honesty. It is also one of the things that get people with Asperger Syndrome into a lot of trouble!

· ·

Case study – Robert

Robert's mum says to him, 'Robert, do you want to have a bath?'

Robert replies, 'Don't be stupid!'

Anyone listening who doesn't know Robert would think he was being incredibly rude to his mum.

The conversation continues:

'Don't call me stupid, Robert!'

'Well, don't be stupid.'

'I'm not being stupid, I just asked if you wanted a bath. Why did you call me stupid?'

'I didn't call you stupid. I just said "don't be stupid". I didn't actually call you stupid.'

'Okay. Well then, why did you imply that I was being stupid? I only asked you if you wanted to have a bath. Why does that make me stupid?'

'It's a stupid thing to ask me.'

'Why?'

'Because I hate having a bath so why would I want to have a bath?'

'Well, what should I have said?'

'Robert, will you have a bath?'

'Okay. Robert, will you have a bath?'

'No.'

'You just said I should say that, and now I've said it you are still arguing about having a bath!'

'I'm not arguing. I haven't been arguing. I am merely correcting you.'

'Correcting me? Look, you need a bath. You haven't had a bath or shower for three days. Go and have a bath, please.'

'Okay.'

It took Robert's mum ages to realize that the words she spoke were of paramount importance to get the desired outcome.

'*Do you want* to have a bath?'

As Robert so bluntly puts it, this is a stupid thing to ask. He hates having a bath so why would he *want* one?

'*Will* you have a bath?'

This gives Robert the option of saying 'no', so he does!

'*Go* and have a bath.'

This instruction is clear and there is no ambiguity. Robert understands straight away what his mum wants from him. Robert's mum doesn't want to seem as though she is ordering Robert about, so she tells him that he must have a bath on that day but he can choose what time he has the bath. As decision making can be very hard for people with autism (see later section), Robert's mum gives him three options – after breakfast, after lunch, or just before bed.

So, Robert's mum managed, eventually, to get the information across to him and also compromised at the same time. Nobody 'won' here. Both parties have been listened to and heard and an agreement has been reached without too much conflict. Of course, it is hard for Robert because he hates having a bath, and it is hard for his mum because, although she knows that Robert didn't mean to be rude and didn't even realize he was being rude, she still feels disrespected and hurt at being called 'stupid'. This is something that Robert and his mum are working on.

From the outside, it could appear that Robert was being rude, but he wasn't. He was just saying what he believed to be the truth of the situation as he saw it. If his mum had got too hung-up on the word 'stupid' and shouted at Robert, or threatened a punishment in that moment, he would have felt that he was being unfairly treated and falsely accused. This would probably have led to a meltdown and created much distress for both Robert and his mum. Robert's mum knows this from experience!

This example illustrates the importance of tone of voice, choice of words, listening and compromise when you are trying to get the best possible outcome for you and your child.

Of course, there will always be times when you can't compromise; for instance, around issues of safety. An example of this might be crossing the road, when you want your child to hold your hand. Scripts, signs and sketches can be really helpful in situations like this.

ASSESS AND MONITOR YOUR OWN BEHAVIOUR

While we spend a lot of time helping our children with their behaviour, it can be just as important to look at our own behaviour and consider its impact on our children. Our response to our children's behaviour can have a massive effect on them, and often the way we behave will dictate our children's next move – will they start to calm down, for example, or will they have a full-blown outburst?

Of course, you are never entirely to blame for your child's behaviour. There are many, many outside influences as we have already discussed. Also, there will always be times when it seems that whatever you do has no effect on your child if he or she is too anxious or too distressed. As a general rule, though, monitor your own behaviour, assess it, and if necessary, change it! Why should it be our children who have to make all of the changes? Just because they are the ones with autism doesn't mean they are the only ones who can display challenging behaviour.

Remember, the transition techniques are there to help you as a family, not to change your child who has autism to suit the rest of the family. Everyone in the family needs to look at their own behaviour and judge the impact this is having on everyone else in the family. The transition techniques will work best in this way – working together as a team with equal thought, care, consideration and respect for everyone.

Case study – Robert

Robert wants to get past his mum in the hallway. As is usual for Robert, he wants to take the direct route. It doesn't occur to him to walk around his mum or to say, 'Excuse me'. Mum is bending down, unplugging the Hoover. Robert just walks past her anyway, makes contact, as there is little space, and Mum is knocked off balance and almost falls over.

There is no intention on Robert's part to be rude here. He really struggles with social and communication skills. He is only focused on his immediate need to get from one end of the hall to the other, and Mum is blocking the way. He doesn't think how his behaviour will affect his mum. He just takes what to him is the most logical action, walks past her and almost knocks her over. He doesn't say sorry.

His mum is taken by surprise and this affects her response. She shouts at Robert:

'Why did you push me over? Couldn't you at least have said "Excuse me"? Why is your need to get past me so urgent that you don't even care if you hurt me?'

That's three questions practically in one breath! A lot of information for Robert to process, and Mum is raising her voice. Robert doesn't think he's done anything wrong.

'I wanted to get past,' he says.

'You could have given me some warning that you were coming past. You could have waited 'til I'd finished unplugging the Hoover and stood up, then there would have been room to get past!'

So much information, spoken quite quickly and loudly. Robert is confused. He shouts back:

'You were in my way!'

'Well, you could have waited a minute. You didn't need to push me over!'

'I didn't push you over. You just fell when I walked past you.'

'Well, if you hadn't walked past me, if you'd waited 'til there was space, I wouldn't have fallen over!'

Mum is really shouting now.

Robert is starting to experience a sensory overload: too many words, too much noise, and he still doesn't realize that he has done something wrong. All of this confusion comes out as anger and Robert starts to have an outburst:

'You're just an idiot, blocking the hallway when I needed to get past!'

'I didn't know you needed to get past!'

'Well, isn't it obvious? How else am I supposed to get upstairs?'

'How was I supposed to know you wanted to get upstairs? And don't call me an idiot!'

'Well, obviously I need to get upstairs if I'm going to my room! Idiot!'

This continues, with both Robert and his mum getting more and more angry. It ends up with Robert putting his hands over his ears and screaming at Mum to, 'Shut up! Just shut up! Shut your mouth, you stupid idiot!'

If you look at this incident from an objective point of view, you can see where Robert's mum went wrong and how her response to his actions triggered negative behaviour in Robert. You can also see how her subsequent response exacerbated this behaviour. We are not blaming his mum, though. She was there, in the moment, dealing with a very difficult situation. Her response was therefore appropriate – appropriate, but not helpful when dealing with the logical mind of her son who has Asperger Syndrome.

Later in the day, when Robert and his mum were calm, they talked about the incident and listened to each other's points of view and how each of them had felt during the argument. It was difficult for Robert to express this because he was confused about his feelings. They found it useful to do sketches of what had actually happened, and what could have happened if they'd both handled the situation differently. It was very much a learning process for both Robert and his mum, and illustrates how our own behaviour and our response to our children's behaviour, can often have an influence on the form and severity of any conflict between us. This is a particularly useful observation to keep in mind during times of change for our children, when they are likely to be anxious, confused and maybe even distressed.

The sketches that Robert and his mum made

Mum and Robert – What actually happened:

Figure 10.1: *What actually happened*

Figure 10.1: What actually happened (continued)

Figure 10.2: What could we have done differently so we both stayed calm?

Figure 10.2: What could we have done differently so we both stayed calm? (continued)

It may be useful to add here that we are well aware that not all negative behaviours can be ignored in the moment; for example, if your child is hurting him- or herself or someone else. You may have to act quickly and just deal with the fallout. Things can be very difficult, and our advice will help you if you use it as often as you can, but obviously this will not always be possible.

CONSEQUENCES FOR NEGATIVE BEHAVIOUR

We all display negative or challenging behaviour at times, not just people with autism, and not just children! Adults can display worse behaviour than children while expecting children to be calm, reasonable, rational and sensible. Of course, in all societies there are consequences for behaviour that is outside the social norm. Sometimes this is a reprimand or exclusion from something; sometimes it is a fine or community work; and ultimately it is a prison sentence. It is important for everyone to understand what is acceptable, and people who have autism are no different. If they are to survive in the neurotypical world, then they need to learn about social rules and boundaries, about what sort of behaviour will get them into trouble, and what the consequences of this behaviour may be.

Agreeing on consequences

We have tried to do this with our son, alongside ignoring, or minimizing our response to, his negative behaviour in the heat of the moment. We have an agreement that goes as follows:

- If Bob is rude or snappy to Mum or Dad, for example, telling Mum to 'shut up', then he is given a warning. If he continues to be rude, he loses his computer time for that day, or the next day if he has already had computer time that day. If he persists in being rude, he is given another warning and reminded that if he carries on he will have to go to bed an hour early.

- If the behaviour does continue, it is likely that Mum or Dad are contributing by responding in a way that is 'winding him up'. We don't mean to take responsibility for his behaviour away from him by saying this; rather, our response, as mentioned earlier, can often dictate our son's next move. We would always try to see how we are contributing to the situation, though this is very hard to do when things are heated.

- If the behaviour continues, then our son would have to go to bed an hour early. We have only got to this point a couple of times because we try to use our strategy of ignoring or minimizing our response to negative behaviour at the time of it happening, so we can deal with it more productively later on.

Ignore, or minimize your reaction to, negative behaviour

Throughout this book we refer to our philosophy of ignoring negative behaviour in the heat of the moment, and dealing with it later, when everyone is calm. Letting things go in the moment can mean the difference between your child calming down and keeping you both safe, or your child's negative behaviour escalating and causing further distress to all concerned.

This strategy can be very difficult to carry out. It is so hard when you are tired, ill or stressed, or in a public place, or in front of friends or family members, or when your child shouts at you, calls you stupid, or tells you to shut up! Of course, we don't always respond calmly to our son, and we always regret that afterwards. So many times we have thought, 'If only I'd let that go until later on, it would have saved so much distress'.

If you want to try this strategy then it is a good idea to do what we did and talk about it first, reach an agreement and write it down. That way you can refer to it if there is any doubt about who agreed to what.

When both you and your child are calm, sit down together and talk about the incident. Try to have an agreement where each person will be given the chance to speak and won't be interrupted or interrupt the other person, even if they don't agree with what the other person is saying. A good way to do this is to use the 'Talking Stick' idea, where an object is passed around from speaker to speaker. The person holding the object (in our case, it was a cuddly lizard!) can speak, uninterrupted, until he or she has finished. The object is then passed to the next person who wishes to speak. It may be a good idea to write down the rules of this strategy so it doesn't end up with people talking forever because they have the item, or snatching the item from the speaker because they themselves want to speak. We have found this to be a very helpful strategy.

Sometimes it helps to write about or draw the issues you are discussing: what happened, how people felt 'in the moment', what other people around you may have thought. We usually find that our son really learns better visually despite his high IQ and so doing sketches and scripts about the disagreement can help him to understand how other people were feeling, and also enable him to understand his own feelings.

Now our son is 16, we may have to think again about how we deal with negative behaviour after the incident, as he is now a young man and so it is going to be much harder to implement consequences! It is therefore now more important than ever to help him to understand about his own feelings and the feelings of other people when there is any conflict. We hope we will get to a point where there don't need to be consequences because he is able to deal with conflict without resorting to name calling or shouting at Mum. He has made great progress but we are not quite 'there' yet!

. . . .

Case study – Bob

Bob was snapping at his mum in a shop and telling her to shut up. They were standing in a busy queue at the time. His mum knew that he was starting to experience a sensory overload and this was the reason for his behaviour, but a woman in the queue said to him, 'You are so rude to your mum!' She continued to rant about his mum letting him 'get away with it…'. Mum left the shop with Bob soon after. At home they talked about how he had been feeling: overwhelmed, anxious, etc.; and how his mum had felt: embarrassed and humiliated. They also talked about why the woman may have responded as she did.

As we have mentioned before, it can be very hard for people with any level of autism to understand and recognize their own feelings, let alone someone else's! This is one of the reasons that the scripts, signs and sketches can be so useful (see Chapter 9 for more detail on how to implement these strategies).

If children respond well to talking about their own feelings, and about their behaviour and the impact it may have on others, then be sure to reward that effort in some way; lots of praise is often enough. We regularly thank our son for all the effort he makes when trying to deal with conflict between us.

Examine your own response to negative behaviour

It is also important to look at how you behaved and how you responded to your child's behaviour. Did you unwittingly instigate or contribute to the incident somehow? Could you have handled it differently so there could have been a more satisfactory outcome? If the answer is 'yes', don't feel guilty, just try to learn from the experience. Our son quite rightly points out that his dad's behaviour is often more infantile and more unreasonable than his, and that he has made massive efforts to change his negative behaviours, so he expects the same from his dad. He has commented that the way Dad snaps at Mum or speaks to her is unacceptable, and far worse than his own communication with Mum; and Mum thinks he may have a point here! Dad has said he will make more effort with his own communication skills, and it is only fair that if our son can work on the incredible challenges that he has in communicating appropriately and effectively, then we should be prepared to do the same.

DECISION MAKING

Decision making can be incredibly stressful for people who have autism, and our son, like many others on the autism spectrum, really struggles to make even the smallest of decisions. Making decisions can be difficult for all of us and most of us find it challenging, even stressful, to make big decisions. However, if you have autism then it is likely that you will feel this level of stress when simply trying to decide if you want to go swimming or to the park, which film to watch, or what to have to eat. We watch our son struggle with these small decisions every day, and we can see the anxiety building in him as he clearly has no idea what to choose. He needs a lot of support when making choices. He will usually say, 'I don't mind', and if we try to take it any further he will get very snappy – it can even lead to an outburst.

One of the ways in which we help him to make decisions is by giving him points on his reward plan for engaging in any part of the decision-making process. For example, he will get points for even trying to weigh up the decision; or for choosing whether or not to go with Mum to visit Grandma and Grandad; or for something as small as deciding which chocolate bar to eat. When we allocate the points, we also explain why he achieved them; for example, 'I have points because I made a decision about whether or not to invite my friend round', or 'I have points because I was able to decide whether to have sausages or bacon with my tea', or 'I have points because I talked things through with Mum and tried to decide if I wanted to go swimming or not. I wasn't able to decide on this occasion but I did at least talk about making the decision – the good things about going and the good things about staying home instead'. He is rewarded for recognizing that there is a decision to be made and for at least acknowledging this, and for trying to make a choice, even if he is not successful.

If you are not doing a reward plan for your child, then you can help your child to make a decision in the following ways:

- Don't give children too many choices in one go; for example, don't say, 'Do you want an apple or a banana or a pear or an orange?' Just give them a choice of two fruits. They may still struggle with making a choice here, but at least you have cut down on some of the anxiety for them.

- Talk through with children the benefits and disadvantages of each option. Try not to overload your children with too much of an explanation as they may get stressed with you talking too much. You could say something like, 'You had a banana after lunch yesterday, so would you like to have an apple today?' That way, you are guiding them towards an answer, but the ultimate decision is theirs. Decision making is quite empowering and they will gain skill and confidence in this process the more you practise with them.

- You can adapt the transition techniques of drawing and writing the information to help children see what the outcome of their choice could be; for example, you could draw a picture of you swimming together and splashing and laughing, to remind them just how much they actually do enjoy swimming.

- You can make a plan or agreement, such as, 'We will only stay in the pool for 15 minutes. If you are starting to feel unhappy we can get out. After our swim we will go to the café for chips', and so on.

This last point can be written as bullet points, or you can do a simple sketch, illustrating each item on your plan; these can be ticked off as they are completed. This helps children feel as though they have some kind of control over what is happening to them. As they know what is coming next at each point, it may help them to relax, and even to make the decision that yes, they would like to go swimming.

As with everything else we talk about in this book, these techniques may not work straight away, and you may need to practise and just keep on trying. Using our reward plan and our scripts, signs and sketches has really helped our son to gain the confidence and skills he needs when it comes to making decisions. He still finds this a difficult process, and it is likely that he always will, but the more he tries the more successful he is, and sometimes now he will make a decision or choice without thinking about it or even realizing that he has done so; in other words, decision making sometimes comes automatically to him, which is, of course, our long-term aim for him.

FLEXIBILITY

People who have autism can struggle significantly with being flexible in their thinking and in their behaviour. Of course, it is this lack of flexibility that leads to individuals struggling with change on every level, but it also affects many other aspects of their lives.

Inflexible thinking can make it very hard indeed for them to see things from another person's point of view, which can lead to all kinds of conflict, and sometimes result in those with autism looking as though they are smug or arrogant, and this is just not the case. One way we try to overcome this with our son is the use of sketches (see Chapter 9, 'Scripts, Signs and Sketches'). We draw a series of pictures which try to explain, for example, what Mum thinks about a certain thing, and why. It may not be what our son thinks, but Mum is entitled to think something different. He really struggles with this concept, but seems to be improving with time and practice.

People with autism can also be extremely inflexible with their behaviour. This is true for everyone to some degree – we all like our routines and don't appreciate them being interrupted! However, for people with autism, an interi their routine can be very anxiety provoking, disrupting everything that makes sense to them and makes them feel safe. This can leave them feeling confused and vulnerable. It is important to recognize that people with autism are probably resorting to rigid behaviour out of some sense of self-preservation, keeping themselves safe from what they view as a daunting and unpredictable world. By seeming not to consider the impact of their behaviour on someone else, they would appear to be thoughtless and selfish, though this is not the case.

An example of inflexible behaviour from our son's life is his adamance that he should cross the road at a certain point. If there is traffic coming, Mum walks along a bit further until the cars have gone and then tries to cross, instead of standing in the same place and waiting for the traffic to move; this just means we are a bit further along with our journey and makes more sense to Mum – it saves time! Our son, however, refuses to walk along and will wait and wait until the cars have gone. He gets really worked up if Mum tries to walk on until there is a break in the traffic, saying something like, 'This is where we cross the road, so get back here!' His behaviour in this situation is so rigid, and Mum knows that if she does continue to walk along and tell him to come with her he will get so wound up, that he will probably start raising his voice to her in the street, and even start name-calling. She knows that he will not care (or even realize) that they are in a public place and that this behaviour is not acceptable. He is so rigid in his thinking in this situation that nothing else seems to matter in that moment, except having Mum do what he wants. He gets very anxious and therefore very angry, and his anger is usually way out of proportion to the situation. This is one of those circumstances where it would be better for Mum to let it go at the time, and try to talk to him and sort it out later. Unfortunately, there is usually something else to deal with by the time they get home, and so this situation has, as yet, gone unresolved, but we really must get around to sorting this out as it happens practically every time he and Mum go out!

All our strategies – the reward plan, transition techniques and scripts, signs and sketches – can be used when dealing with inflexible behaviour. We have used them successfully in many situations with our son when his rigid thinking or inflexible behaviour have been preventing all of us getting on with our lives. They have helped him not only to become more flexible, but to be more open to recognizing those situations when he isn't being flexible, and trying to address this.

YOU FEEL YOU'VE TRIED EVERYTHING
– AND NOTHING WORKS

> They say, 'Try this, try that!' Well, I've tried everything and nothing works…
>
> (Mother of a daughter with autism)

All parents and carers of people affected by autism have probably got to this point at some time, probably several times, if we are honest! The neurological make-up of neurotypical people and that of people with an autism spectrum condition seem to be so different that it should come as no great surprise that we often fail to understand each other or to communicate effectively. We take advice from many sources, try it ourselves and often feel like failures if it has no effect on the challenging behaviour of our children with autism. You will probably feel like giving up, and find yourself wondering, 'What's the point?' If you have ever felt like this, don't feel guilty or as though you are letting your child down in some way. You are not the first person to feel like this, and will certainly not be the last. We all feel this way sometimes, especially if we are sleep-deprived or trying to cope alone. It is so painful to see our children struggling with the things other people's children seem to be 'sailing' through. You may have financial problems, relationship issues, difficulties at work or challenges brought on by your other, neurotypical children. The contributing factors to our own stress levels vary greatly, and can have a massive impact on our abilities to cope with the challenges thrown up by autism.

Seek help

It is important not to be afraid to seek help. This might be help for your child or it may be help for you as an individual. You may need practical help, emotional support or financial assistance. Try to seek out whatever it is you think might help you feel better, and therefore enable you to support your child more effectively. If you are not sure how or where to go for help, see the Resource section at the back of this book for ideas.

Obtain a diagnosis

Some people are reluctant to get a diagnosis for their child because they feel that this is a label and something that will stay with their child forever. They fear that it will be on record for all time, and available for medical, insurance, educational and employment agencies and individuals to read and therefore judge their child by. To some degree this point is difficult to argue with. We have argued it, however, with other home educating parents, who made us feel that we had let our son down in some way by seeking a diagnosis and getting professional support when we were way out of our depth with his outbursts. We didn't tell them about our son's outbursts or any other personal information about him, and only told a handful of people about his autism diagnosis, but those people judged us instead of supporting us, and made us feel inadequate both as parents and as home educators.

However, autism is not a label; it is a diagnosis, a neurological difference that may need to be identified in order to provide appropriate support. Whether or not to get a diagnosis is very much up to the parents or carers to decide. It can also be up to the individual who may have autism, if he or she is able to make an informed choice about this. When your children are aware of their diagnosis, they may feel very empowered. They may have been wondering why they were different and didn't fit in with the majority of other children; they were probably thinking that there was something wrong with them. Once they are diagnosed as having a neurological difference, many of those children start to feel better, more in control. This was certainly the case with our son. While it is possible for many of the autistic symptoms, such as meltdowns, to disappear once children are taken out of the overwhelming environment of school to become home educated (and this was partly true for our son), they may still need to know why they are finding life so difficult. Lots of parents, home educating or not, do choose to seek a diagnosis for their child.

It is very much up to you, but if you are struggling with your child and you know or suspect that he or she has autism spectrum condition, then don't be afraid to ask for some professional advice and support. After an initial struggle to get the support our son needed, we then had a very positive experience with his psychologist, speech and language therapist, physiotherapist and occupational therapist. Getting the services was not easy, but they were well worth waiting for. Unfortunately, our experience is not the case for all families we know of. Many of them have not been happy with the services they have been offered, or with the individual providing the service. It is important to have a good working relationship with any professional who is involved in your child's care, and if this is not so, then you may need to make some attempts to change this. It can be difficult to be assertive enough to challenge professionals, but if you do it politely and calmly, you may well get the outcome you want to ensure that you and your child are getting the support you need.

Gather your strength and try again

If you have tried the advice and techniques recommended by any professionals involved in your child's life, and you have tried lots of strategies that you have learned elsewhere (e.g., from books like this), and you *still* feel you are getting nowhere, it can be helpful to take a step back and look at what you have tried. How did you go about it? Were you consistent enough with your approach? Did you try the new technique or strategy for long enough? This is not intended as a criticism; it's just that any change in your child's behaviour can be a very slow process, requiring lots of time, energy, consistency and patience on your part. This can feel very hard and often impossible, especially if you are coping on your own. Sadly, we often have to get through the negative side of autism to allow ourselves and our children to recognize and even enjoy the positive side. Perhaps you could consider re-trying some of the things you have already tried, but this time plan carefully and be really prepared, focused and consistent.

We created a really positive reward plan for our son when we were dealing with some very aggressive outbursts, and this was a massive success. However, it didn't happen overnight and took a lot of hard work and consistency on our part (see *Create a Reward Plan for Your Child with Asperger Syndrome*). We can't emphasize enough how important it is to stick with things no matter how hard it gets. Sometimes things do get harder for a while before they get easier. If you are working through some difficult issues with your child who has autism, try to get some support for yourself while you are doing this. The support may come from family, friends, a counsellor, your child's psychologist, a group specially formed to provide help and advice for people affected by autism, an organization such as the National Autistic Society, or some other source. Take care not to isolate yourself – this is so easy to do and so difficult to undo.

None of the above is meant to make you feel like an inadequate parent, while we have all the answers – we certainly don't, and we still struggle on a regular basis with our son's autism. We have, however, been lucky enough to develop, implement and maintain some strategies that have really worked for us as a family. However, we are always facing new challenges and asking ourselves, 'Will our techniques work with this? Do we need to develop further techniques to deal with this issue?' In other words, the work we do as a family to help us to deal with the negative side of our son's autism, so we can get the chance to appreciate the good things, is an ongoing project. While we still make some major mistakes that directly affect our son and his ability to deal with stress, it is probably safe to say that we are more skilled now in recognizing and dealing with problems as they arise.

Points to remember:

- It might be worth seeking the advice of someone who specializes in autism, if you haven't already.

- Have a re-think about the strategies you have already tried and decide if it would be worth trying them again, this time for longer and with more consistency.

- Think about what you need to help *you*, not just your child. Try to work out if and how you can get this help.

- Above all, don't blame yourself for the lack of progress made by your son or daughter when trying out strategies or techniques to help with a particular issue. The main thing is that you are trying to help your child, and it may simply be that you need a little support to do this.

General advice from Bob

For parents

LISTEN

Most important, you should always listen to your child, even if you think he or she is talking nonsense. Just because something isn't important to you doesn't mean that it isn't important to someone else! If you listen to your child, you are also setting a good example, which will encourage them to listen to you, and to other people.

Listening is a skill; it isn't just about hearing what people have to say and going, 'yeah, yeah…'. Listening is about taking notice of what those people say, of what they think, and taking them seriously, even if it is something you consider trivial or insignificant. You don't have to agree with what people are saying, but you do need to give them space to say it, to express themselves, not to constantly interrupt or talk over them or try to finish their sentences for them. That's just irritating!

BE PATIENT WHEN YOUR CHILD DOESN'T UNDERSTAND SOCIAL ETIQUETTE

Remember that social situations may be confusing for your child, and he or she won't necessarily see things the same way you do. You may need to be patient when your child's behaviour doesn't meet the social etiquette. An example of this in my life is queuing for buses: I have never understood the social rules surrounding this. One minute Mum tells me that the person at the front of the queue gets on the bus first, and then she lets other people on before us, because they are elderly or have an obvious physical disability and are struggling, or the person may be pregnant, or have young children or lots of shopping, and so on! I think this is really unfair, especially as we often have to wait ages for a bus. I understand that some people may have more need of a seat than me, but I still find the whole situation very confusing. In the past, I have become angry at the bus stop because of this, and people have blamed my behaviour on Mum, saying she's a 'bad' mum. People don't seem to understand that for some of us the social rules don't make any sense and leave us confused and frustrated. This is one situation where Mum and I have to listen to each other. I accept Mum's guidance in this situation, as I know my lack of acceptance here has got us into trouble in the past. I do as Mum asks but then, at other times (when we are not at the bus stop!) I do like to have a good 'rant' about the unfairness of it all!

KEEP CALM

Most things can be sorted out by talking to each other, but once people get angry and start shouting, it becomes really hard to reach an agreement. IF YOUR CHILD IS NOT CALM THEN YOU NEED TO BE. This is easier said than done, I know, but just do your best!

In the past, when Mum and I have had arguments, we have noticed that if she has got angry and started raising her voice, and it has gone on like that with each of us winding the other one up, these arguments seem to be longer, more drawn out and more unpleasant than when Mum has stayed calm.

DON'T OVERLOAD YOUR CHILD

Don't overload your child with too much information at once; for example, don't give too many instructions. If children tell you to be quiet or to shut up, they probably don't mean to be rude, they just can't stand to hear your voice any more in that moment! Don't take this personally. It is more likely that they are starting to experience a sensory overload and just need some quiet.

Sometimes, when too much information or too much talking leads to sensory overload, it can in turn lead to an outburst, and then to conflict, so this is obviously best avoided.

Bob's comments

For young people with autism

TRY TO COMMUNICATE HOW YOU ARE FEELING

However small a change may be, it can still have a massive effect on a household with a child who has autism. One of the main problems isn't how people with autism react to a change, although this is definitely a problem, but rather, the fact that the people around them, who don't have autism, have no way of knowing the effect this change has on them. This is why it is so important that you try to communicate how you are feeling about changes that are coming up, even though you might find it hard to talk about things.

You may even feel embarrassed that you react so strongly to what others see as minor changes. If people don't know that you are finding things hard, they won't be able to help you, and your behaviour may seem erratic and inexcusable. However, if they know what the reason for it is, they are much more likely to try to help you with it, rather than just grow angry with you about it.

You can use signs to try to help you communicate your feelings about change (see Chapter 9, 'Scripts, Signs and Sketches'). Try not to be nervous about talking to people – sometimes it's hard for people with autism to recognize how they are actually feeling. It may be helpful for you to read Chapter 3, 'Emotions'.

BE PREPARED TO TRY NEW STRATEGIES

Another important thing is that you have to be prepared to try anything in order to avoid the problems that come with these changes. However silly or pointless it may seem, it's always worth trying, and if it happens to work it will save you a lot of trouble in the long run. If you use some of the techniques in this book and they suit you, then before you know it, changes will be going by on a daily basis, and you won't even be noticing them.

THINKING AHEAD

Another good technique for getting through change, or just any stressful time, is thinking ahead to when it's over. For example, if you wake up and you know you have a big change or something stressful that day, or you know that at, say, two o'clock you will have to do something you don't want to do, don't think, 'It's only five hours until I have to do that'; instead think, 'It's only six hours until that's over!'

ON A FINAL NOTE

We hope that you find this general advice useful. It can be very helpful when dealing with issues around change and transition, as well as other difficult areas in your child's life, and in your relationship with your child. This chapter presents just a selection of issues that we know can create challenges for you and your child. Of course, there is a whole host of other examples we could have used; you can probably think of loads from your own life. The point we are trying to get across really is that the techniques and strategies we offer in this book and in our previous book can be used for the many issues we have raised; but you can also take them, adapt them and use them for most of the problems that life will throw at you and your child. If you take some time out to read about them and practise them, you should find it easier to apply them when you need to.

It is important that you don't try to change your child too much! We hope our techniques will offer you and your child strategies to work together to help you as a family come through some of the challenges autism brings, so you can focus more on the positive things about your child. We can't emphasize enough that this book isn't about curing your child of autism. It is about embracing your child's autism, which isn't always easy to do! If you use the transition techniques we offer in this book, the transition through times of change should be smoother for your child, and allow you all more time and energy to concentrate on the more pleasant aspects of your life together.

Put in the work and be consistent

It has already been said in this book (probably several times) that the hardest part of dealing with the difficulties you face regarding your child's autism is being consistent. If you can be consistent with the techniques and strategies we are inviting you to share, you will have much greater success than if you try things intermittently and give up too soon. It's a bit like trying to lose weight; if you try one of the many diets on offer and do some exercise, this may work for you, but at times you will feel like it's not working any more or not working quickly enough. Our advice, with both dieting and parenting, is to avoid trends and quick fixes. In both cases, it's about making a positive choice about your life-style, and being consistent with that. Life-long changes are a lot harder to achieve, but if you think about what you are doing now, you have to ask yourself, 'Is it working for me?' If it isn't, then you need to make those changes and stick to them! It's hard, but worth it, and no one else can do it for you. Professionals can help but they don't have the same emotional investment in your child that you have, and they have lots of other children to deal with. If you want to help your child and your family as a whole, then you will have to put the work in – and keep on putting the work in.

Dealing with burn out

And you will need to deal with this. We have. In fact, during the writing of this book, Mum is actually struggling with depression and finding it very hard to be consistent in continuing with the strategies and techniques we are using with our son. We keep going because we know how things were before we developed our reward plan, transition techniques, and scripts, signs and sketches. And yes, life is a struggle at the moment, but we never want to go back to those days. It would be so hard for us and even harder for our son.

If you do find yourself starting to 'burn out', then try really hard to take some time out for yourself. Of course, we know how difficult this is, especially if you are a single parent, or if you are trying to cope with the demands of work or caring for other children as well for as your child with autism. When you become a parent, you can start to lose your own identity – this is probably more true for mothers; when you have a child with autism, this loss of identity can be even more pronounced and will possibly last for a lot longer, maybe even continuing when your child is an adult. We need to be careful to avoid this as much as possible. It is a fact that if you take good care of yourself you will be better able to take good care of your child. The problem is finding the time (and the energy) to look after your own needs when your every waking moment is taken up with thoughts of, and care for, your child.

If you are part of a couple, then it is also very important to take care of your relationship. If you neglect each other, you are less likely to stay together and this will have an impact on the whole family. You may be the parent of a child with autism, but you are so much more than that – you are still an individual, part of a couple, a friend and so on. Try to make time for your relationships outside of your child, and you will probably find that your relationship with your child improves. You may be reading this and thinking, 'Well, that's easy for them to say!' It isn't. Remember, we are talking from experience; we are separated and have been for nearly nine years at the writing of this book. Mum has been through complete isolation and had to work very hard to come back from this. Maintaining relationships, and especially building new ones, is very difficult indeed, but we have to try. We owe it to ourselves and our children, because it is a much healthier situation to be in, and more 'normal'. We will make better role models for our children if they see us as whole, well-rounded, independent individuals, and not just as an extension of themselves – which is how our son saw Mum for many years!

Helpful tips to avoid burn out

- Try to make some time for yourself, doing something you find fun or relaxing. That may be going out for a drink with a friend or even just walking the dog by yourself. You need some time to think your own thoughts in your own head without constant interruption.

- If you are part of a couple, try to schedule some time for each of you to do something you like while the other one takes care of the children. Write this on a calendar or in a diary and stick to it!

- If you are a single parent, try to find someone you can trust with your child who is prepared to care for him or her, say once a week, so you can have some 'me time'. You may have to build this up over a period of time so your child can get used to this change. Use the transition techniques to help you do this.

- You don't even have to go out. Sometimes it would just be lovely to have an uninterrupted bath!

- If you are a couple, try your best to have some quality 'couple time' when someone else looks after the children. You could do something relaxing, something fun, or both! Don't spend the whole time talking about the children and phoning home constantly! Try to switch off from everything but each other.

- If you really don't have a friend or family member to help you, maybe you could contact your local autism support group, as they often have 'buddy' schemes and they may be able to help.

- Money is often an issue for families who have a child with specific or additional needs (notice we don't say 'special' as we think that sounds really patronizing), but you don't have to spend money to have some time to yourself. You can go to visit family or friends, go for a walk, or even just have some time in a different room reading. Or it may be that it's your children that leave the house, and you can put your feet up and watch TV.

However you choose to spend your 'me time' is up to you, but please do try to have some.

That's enough general advice from us. We hope there is something here that you can take away and use in your own life. All of the techniques and strategies we talk about have helped us enormously and they could help you too. We wish you the very best of luck.

CONCLUSION

Throughout this book we have shown that change, however small, can impact on our children and affect their emotions and behaviour to varying degrees.

We have also demonstrated techniques we use as a family to help to minimize the negative issues that arise surrounding times of change and transition.

Change cannot be avoided. To constantly avoid change wherever possible will make it all the harder for our children to deal with change that can`t be eschewed. Change is such a big and consistent part of all our lives, and so our children need to learn how to deal with it to the best of their ability. This is why our transition techniques can be so helpful – they break down each situation and simplify it to a level that our children can understand and work with.

The more we practise using the transition techniques, the easier they become to use. This can be particularly helpful when faced with an unexpected change for which we haven`t had a chance to prepare our children.

There are no short cuts or easy fixes when dealing with any of the challenges that autism brings. There are so many positive things about our son`s Asperger Syndrome: his intelligence, sense of humour and loyalty, to name a few; but often the negative side of his Asperger Syndrome can get in the way of this. The transition techniques, reward plan and scripts, signs and sketches we developed are all designed to help our son deal with the downside of his autism so he is then more able to embrace the upside.

In *Create a Reward Plan for your Child with Asperger Syndrome* we emphasize that we are not trying to change who Bob is, to cure him, or even make him less autistic. The idea is to get the best out of his autism while helping him to `get-by` in the neurotypical world at the same time. We hope this will make his life less stressful and less confusing.

All the techniques we use with our son have helped us immensely as a family, which is why we wrote the first book, and why we have now written this one. If we share our techniques and strategies with other families that are affected by autism, then maybe those families will benefit from our experience and have the same positive outcome that we have had.

Since using the reward plan, the scripts, signs and sketches and the transition techniques, we have seen our son develop in every area of his life. We have all had to work very hard, no one more so than him. And we have had to be consistent with the techniques, when at times it felt easier just to give up. But you can`t give up on your child with autism, and you can`t always look to professionals to provide all the help your child may need. Often it takes too long to get an appointment, and you may not get support for as long as you need it because of the huge demand on resources. It can be very beneficial to have professional people involved in your child`s life, but if you can also work with your child at home, on a daily basis, you will back up any work you are doing with doctors, psychologists, teachers and so on, and provide your child with the input he or she needs on a day-to-day basis.

Our son has struggled, and may always struggle, with all areas of social and communication skills, decision making, and initiating social interaction or activities. He may always find these aspects of his life challenging and he may continue to need support in these areas – only time will tell. However, we are fully confident that the strategies and techniques we have developed as a family, along with as the services he has received from his psychologist, speech therapist, physiotherapist and occupational therapist (you know who you are – thank you!), have improved his life significantly over the past few years.

Bob now has far greater skills in all areas of his life. His confidence and self-esteem have been given a real boost as he realizes more and more just what he is capable of, and that his autism – though a huge part of his life, and often a very positive part – doesn`t define him as a person. He now knows that he has choices, and that the more effort he puts into his life the more he will get out of it

Our son has worked incredibly hard using the techniques and strategies described in this book, and in our reward plan book. He couldn`t try any harder than he does and we are very, very proud of him. We believe he is a brilliant example and role model for young people who are affected by autism. He is also a wonderful role model for anyone who finds life challenging, and needs some advice or support to try their best to face those challenges, work with them, make the best of them and move on from them. It is possible to move on to new and more positive challenges, as did Bob, who started college full time when he was still only fifteen.

We sincerely hope that you have enjoyed reading this book, and that our transition techniques and the additional techniques we use to support these, have been of interest to you. We hope they will be of some use to you and your family. Give them a try!

USEFUL RESOURCES

Throughout this book we have made reference to various issues and subjects, such as dyslexia and home education.

This section of the book has been written to direct you to resources that can help you to gain more knowledge on each of these topics, or to find the help that you may need for yourself and your child.

It can be very frustrating not knowing where to go or who to turn to when you are struggling with a situation or a problem, and often there is somewhere you can go to get the help that you need, if only you knew where!

We have written a section for each of the topics and then provided some details of organizations that may be able to help with each one. We have tried to do this for each of the countries in which this book will be available.

There are email addresses and websites, and phone numbers for those of you who don't have access to the internet.

Have a read through and see if there is anything of interest here for you. If not, just keep this resource section in mind, as you never know what may come up in the future.

AUTISM/ASPERGER SYNDROME
USA
AutismUSA.net
www.autismusa.net
Tel: + 917 734 8936
Email: atlas@autismusa.net
Information resource on autism and other developmental conditions. Contains links to internet resources and websites.

Autism Society
4340 East-West Hwy
Suite 350
Bethesda
Maryland 20814
www.autism-society.org
Tel: + 301 657 0881
Email direct from the site.
Information and advice on autism.

Canada
Autism Society Canada
Box 22017
1670 Heron Road
Ottawa
Ontario
K1V OC2
www.autismsocietycanada.ca
Tel: + 613 789 8943
Email: info@autismsocietycanada.ca
Information and advice on autism.

UK
The National Autistic Society
393 City Road
London
EC1V 1NG
www.autism.org.uk
Tel: +44 (0) 20 7833 2299
Email: nas@nas.org.uk
Information and support on all aspects of autism.

DYSLEXIA
USA
Dyslexia USA
www.dyslexia-usa.com
This provides links to dyslexia websites for all of the states and territories so there is no actual phone number or email for the main site, but each link has its own contact details. If you don't have access to email you may have to use a library or internet café just to get the initial details. The links provide information and advice regarding dyslexia.

Canada

Canadian Dyslexia Association

57 Rue du Couvent
Gatineau
Quebec
JH9 3C8
www.dyslexiaassociation.ca
Tel: + 613 853 6539
Email: info@dy

Dyslexia Canada

Ottawa Office
290 Picton Avenue
Ottawa
Ontario
K1Z 8P8
Tel: + 613 722 2699
Email: cda@ottawa.com
This site provides advice and information regarding dyslexia.

UK

British Dyslexia Association

Unit 8
Bracknell Beeches
Old Bracknell Lane
Bracknell
Berkshire
RG12 7BW
www.bdadyslexia.org.uk
Tel: +44 (0)845 251 9003
Email: helpline@bdadyslexia.org.uk
This site provides help and advice on dyslexia.

Dyslexia Action

Park House
Wick Road
Egham
Surrey
TW20 OHH
Tel: +44 (0)1784 222 300
Email direct from site.
This site provides help and advice on dyslexia.

DYSPRAXIA

USA

Dyspraxia Foundation USA
3059 N. Lincoln Ave
Unit C
Chicago
Illinois 60657
www.dyspraxiausa.org
Tel: + 312 496 6635
Email direct from site.
Provides information and advice on dyspraxia.

Canada

AQED (Association Quebecoise pour les enfants dyspraxic – Canada)
CP 26024
Sherbrooke
Quebec
Canada
J1G 4J9
Tel: +819 829 0594
Email: dyspraxie@sympatico.ca
Provides information and advice on dyspraxia.

UK

Dyspraxia Foundation
8 West Alley
Hitchin
Hertfordshire
SG5 1EG
www.dyspraxiafoundation.org.uk
Tel: +44 (0)1462 454 986
Email: dyspraxia@dyspraxiafoundation.org.uk
This site offers support, advice and links to other useful websites.

Dyspraxic Teens
www.dyspraxicteens.org.uk
This site offers advice and resource information, and has chat forums and a message board.

HOME EDUCATION

USA

Homeschooling in America

www.homeschoolinginamerica.com

This site offers advice and information regarding home schooling in each of the American states.

Canada

Canadian Home Based Learning Resource Page

www.flora.org/homeschool-ca

Email direct from site.

This site offers advice and information regarding home schooling.

UK

Education Otherwise

PO Box 3761

Swindon

Wiltshire

SN2 9GT

www.education-otherwise.net

Tel: +44 (0)845 478 6345

Email direct from site.

HEAS

Home Education Advisory Service

PO Box 98

Welwyn Garden City

Hertfordshire

AL8 6AN

www.heas.org.uk

Tel: +44 (0) 1707 371 854

Email: enquiries@heas.org.uk

Advice and practical support for families wishing to home educate.

TOURETTE'S SYNDROME

USA

Tourette Syndrome Association
42–40 Bell Blvd
Bayside
New York 11361
www.tsa-usa.org
Tel: + 718 224 2999
Email direct from site.
Information and support regarding all aspects of Tourette's Syndrome.

Canada

TSFC
Tourette Syndrome Foundation of Canada
5945 Airport Rd
Suite 195
Mississauga
Ontario
L4V 1R9
www.tourette.ca
Tel: + 905 673 2255
Email direct from site.

UK

Tourettes Action
Kings Court
91–93 High Street
Camberley
Surrey
GU15 3RN
www.tourettes-action.org.uk
Tel: +44 (0)1276 482 903
Email: admin@tourettes-action.org.uk
A charity working to make life better for people with Tourette's Syndrome.

FINANCIAL HELP

USA

MAINST

www.mainstreet.com

This site gives links to organizations that provide grants to families affected by autism including: The National Autism Association; Autism Speaks; Autism Society of America; ACT today; NeighborHeart; Autism Cares.

You will need to find the Mainstreet site using a search engine before you can access the links.

Canada

AACF

Autism Support Network & Aid for Autistic Children Foundation, Inc. Create Alliance to help families affected by autism.

Contact: Karen Lee

Email: Karen.lee@aacfinc.org

This organization provides financial advice and support.

UK

The National Autistic Society

393 City Road

London

EC1V 1NG

www.autism.org.uk

Tel: +44 (0)207 833 2299

Email: nas@nas.org.uk

This site has a section giving advice and contact details for applying for financial assistance. Click on 'benefits and community care' from the home page.

We hope that you find these resources useful. It is always worth taking a look to see if there is any way in which any of the above organizations can help you. This is just a selection, and if you have access to the internet you may be able to find additional sites that will be of interest to you.